Praise for *The C*
Guide to the Gr

Erin MacPherson has covered ALL the bases in *The Christian Mama's Guide to the Grade School Years,* an exceptional guidebook for parents. Tackling difficult topics such as bullying, extracurricular activities, and helicopter parenting, this faith-based guide will become the go-to source for any parent who hopes to help children navigate this great big world while keeping their little souls intact.

—JULIE CANTRELL, *NEW YORK TIMES* BEST-SELLING
AUTHOR OF *INTO THE FREE, GOD IS WITH ME THROUGH
THE DAY,* AND *GOD IS WITH ME THROUGH THE NIGHT*

The Christian Mama's Guide to the Grade School Years is a must-have resource for every Christian mom who wants to give her child the best and not lose her sanity in the process. With authenticity and wit, MacPherson tackles the tough questions of parenting and gives readers a practical road map for grace-based parenting. MacPherson doesn't give easy answers or a "one-size-fits-all" approach to raising kids. Instead, she gives practical examples, grace, and generational wisdom to equip the mothers of our generation. I recommend this book to every Christian mom of grade-school children!

—SUSAN DiMICKELE, AUTHOR OF *WORKING
WOMEN OF THE BIBLE* AND *CHASING SUPERWOMAN*

This book is hands-down fabulous! Erin covers all the bases with this guide to success in school and life with a commitment to faith in God as the core. Depth and perspective comes from the practical advice of Erin's mother, a veteran mom and school principal. Erin's personal life experiences mingled with teachable moments, scripture, prayer, and a huge dose of humor make this a must-read book for Christian parents. As a former elementary school teacher and mom, I highly recommend *The Christian Mama's Guide to the Grade School Years.*

—BECKY DANIELSON, MED, LICENSED PARENT
AND FAMILY EDUCATOR AND COAUTHOR OF
EMPOWERED PARENTS: PUTTING FAITH FIRST

Erin MacPherson has written a parenting book that is engaging, delightful, and humorous and most importantly, offers excellent insight in helping parents enrich their children spiritually in a very easy, relatable way.

—JORDYN REDWOOD, PEDIATRIC ER NURSE
AND AUTHOR OF *PROOF* AND *POISON*

What every mom needs as she holds her child's hand on the way to drop him off to school for the first time, is another mom holding her *other* hand, assuring her that everything will be okay. Erin is just that reassuring mom-companion. Armed with experience, practical tips, empathy, humor, and a backpack of prayer, Erin MacPherson's indispensable guide will help you parent your child in the early school years with confidence and faith.

—BECKY JOHNSON, COAUTHOR OF
WE LAUGH, WE CRY, WE COOK

As mothers who've experienced sending their children off to school, we all know how taxing this milestone can be. Most of us become fraught with worry (and get downright emotional) as we struggle with the idea of having to let go, and face the fact that our babies are indeed growing up. But as Erin MacPherson so eloquently discusses throughout *The Christian Mama's Guide to the Grade School Years*, these are the moments where moms like us can place our trust in God and His plans for our children's future. This is the time where we can step out in our faith, and send our struggles straight up to Him. And as a mom who definitely understands what battling those "back-to-school blues" are all about, MacPherson equips each of her readers with loads of practical advice, invaluable information, beautifully scripted (not to mention, reassuring) words of faith, and plenty of comic relief to go around. So, if you've got kiddos headed off to school soon (or even if they've begun their elementary days already), be sure to arm yourself with this book. You'll be so glad you did.

—JENNY LEE SULPIZIO, AUTHOR OF
CONFESSIONS OF A WONDER WOMAN WANNABE

Oh, how we needed this book two decades ago when the "self-esteem movement" was brainwashing parents into raising generations of entitled kids! Erin's Fifteen Factors are spot-on remedies for the spiritual immaturity and arrested social development I see daily in my high school students. With hilarious transparency, keen insights, and practical faith, Erin coaches you to support and challenge your child without enabling or over-protecting. Chapter 14 alone—"Do This, Not That"—is worth the price of admission!

—CHERI GREGORY, VETERAN TEACHER, AUTHOR, AND
FOUNDER OF THE PURSE-ONALITY CHALLENGE MINISTRY

THE
CHRISTIAN
MAMA'S
GUIDE
TO THE GRADE SCHOOL YEARS

Other Books by Erin MacPherson

The Christian Mama's Guide to Having a Baby
The Christian Mama's Guide to Baby's First Year
The Christian Mama's Guide to Parenting a Toddler

THE
CHRISTIAN MAMA'S GUIDE

TO THE GRADE SCHOOL YEARS

Everything You

Need to Know to

Survive (*and Love*)

Sending Your Kid off

into the Big, Wide World

ERIN MACPHERSON

THOMAS NELSON

Since 1798

NASHVILLE   DALLAS   MEXICO CITY   RIO DE JANEIRO

Published in Nashville, Tennessee, by Thomas Nelson. Thomas Nelson is a registered trademark of Thomas Nelson, Inc.

Author is represented by Books & Such Literary Agency.

Thomas Nelson, Inc., titles may be purchased in bulk for educational, business, fundraising, or sales promotional use. For information, please e-mail SpecialMarkets@ThomasNelson.com.

Unless otherwise noted, Scripture references are taken from the Holy Bible, New International Version®, NIV®. Copyright © 1973, 1978, 1984, 2011 by Biblica, Inc.™ Used by permission of Zondervan. All rights reserved worldwide. www.zondervan.com

Scripture references marked NKJV are taken from THE NEW KING JAMES VERSION. © 1982 by Thomas Nelson, Inc. Used by permission. All rights reserved.

Library of Congress Control Number: 2013930851

ISBN: 9780849964763

Printed in the United States of America

13 14 15 16 17 RRD 6 5 4 3 2 1

To my wonderful and wise parents,
Glen and Ellen Schuknecht,
who patiently answer my parenting
questions, cheer me on from the sidelines,
and pray without ceasing for my family.

Contents

Acknowledgments

*S*oli *Deo Gloria*. To God alone be the glory. That's my prayer for this book. I am acutely aware of the fact that every good gift comes from the Lord, and I am eternally grateful for everything He has given me—I am so blessed.

This book wouldn't have happened without the insights, ideas, and support of my incredibly wise parents, Glen and Ellen Schuknecht. I appreciate the many hours they spent sitting with me at their kitchen counter, discussing ideas, strategies, and thoughts about this book. I am so grateful not only for their wisdom, but also for their dedicated prayer and their willingness to coach parents everywhere on how to raise kids that love God.

My heartfelt gratitude also goes to my husband, Cameron, who is the most amazing father my kids could ask for. He has stepped up to the plate—literally—and been the kind of dad who plays catch, teaches them how to build pillow forts, and most important, teaches them about God. I'm proud to raise my kids with you.

And to my own grade-school-aged kids, Joey and Kate, I thank you for allowing me to "test" out my theories on you and for being patient with me as I learn with you. And to my baby, Will, who isn't quite there yet, thank you for the endless laughter and endless hugs.

Also, to Alisa, who once again stepped up to the plate and read this entire book for edits and was quick to share her brilliance with me as I fit the pieces together. Thanks also to Troy, who shared endless daddy insight. And also, a big thanks to my other grade-school mom friends—Mollie Burpo, Kat Cannon, Kristin Cox, Angie Ekse, Mandy Fritsche, Joanne Kraft, Hollie Rouse, Monica Scantlon,

Stevi Schuknecht, and Rachel Spies, to name a few, for letting me quiz you on how you're raising your kids, and then publish what you say for the world to see. You are such great moms, and I'm proud to raise my kids alongside you.

And last, but certainly not least, thank you to the amazing team at Thomas Nelson, along with my agent, Rachelle Gardner, who have truly gone above and beyond to help me get these books written and published. I appreciate you.

Introduction

Into the Big, Wide (and Sometimes Scary) World

Whoever created the drop-off policy at my son Joey's elementary school had clearly never met a newbie kindergarten mom. Because when the letter outlining first-day drop-off instructions arrived in the mail along with his school supply list, I started to hyperventilate. Okay, so I might be exaggerating, but I certainly had a momentary panic when I considered whiting out my son's birth date on his birth certificate and keeping him home another year.

The letter was short and sweet.

> Dear Parents,
>
> In an effort to ensure the safety of our students on the first day of school, we ask that you drop all kids off by the front doors and then continue to exit through the west parking lot. We will have teachers and student leaders available to escort new kindergarten students through the doors and into the cafeteria where their teachers will be waiting. We ask that you please do not park your car in order to walk your child into the school...

That's all I had to read for the panic to start. My son—*my baby!*—had to walk from my car and into the big, wide school all by himself.

All. By. Himself. What if his backpack was too heavy? Or what if a big, bad fifth grader bullied him as he walked in? (I hear those big kids are getting bigger every year.) I mean, the potential crises that could result in those ten steps between my car and the school were enough to make my heart start a-racin'. He could stub his toe as he walked through the threshold, for goodness' sake, and spend the entire day in toe-stubbed misery. This was not good. Not good at all.

As terrible scenarios raced through my mind, my husband had to restrain me from picking up the phone and calling the school to complain. He reminded me that schools make policies like that for a reason. And usually that reason was because of over-panicky parents like me. Okay, he didn't say that. But I could tell he was thinking it.

On the Saturday before school started, we drove to the school and practiced. (I know, I know. Overachiever mom. Or maybe it's overprotective mom.) I pulled up in front of the school and let Joey unbuckle himself, grab his backpack, and walk those ten big steps to the door. He did it five times—just for good measure—and once I was confident that he was going to manage just fine without stubbing his toe, we left.

And on Monday, I put on my bravest face.

I scrubbed Joey's face and combed his hair. I made pancakes for breakfast and arranged blueberries in the shape of a smiley face on top. I lovingly packed his lunch and wrote him a little note just to say how much I adored him (because I figured he'd be reading by lunchtime; he's supersmart). I took at least ten thousand pictures before I loaded him into the car. And I put those keys in the ignition and headed toward the school while trying to control the tears that threatened to start rolling down my face.

As we pulled up to the school, I pasted a smile on my face as I turned to my baby-turned-big boy and said "This is it, Joey! I'm so proud of you! I love you."

And he was off.

Confidently taking those first ten steps into the big, wide world.

I watched him take every single one of those steps in my rearview mirror with tears streaming down my face. Tears of joy. Tears of sadness. And tears of hope. And I prayed that as we all made this big—no, monumental—transition of starting school, I could handle it with courage, grace, and a giant sprinkling of Christlike love.

Sending your baby off into the big, wide world is bittersweet. It's exciting. Your kid now has the chance to make a stand—a stand for who he is, what he believes in, and what he wants to be. But it's also sad. Your baby is growing up. And while this is certainly not the end of your time as a mom—you can go ahead and trust me that your mom skills will be tested in the year to come as they've never have been before—it's the end of an era of sorts. And as you move out of the preschool era, you get to move into the big-kid era.

An era when your kid will grow and learn more than you ever imagined.

An era when your kid will (hopefully) solidify his trust in Christ.

An era when your kid will learn what faith and grace and hope truly mean.

And as you make this transition, I want to come beside you to share my stories. My struggles. My over-panicky moments. So that you, too, can send your kid off into the big, wide world with the confidence he needs to thrive.

*A note for my particularly scrupulous readers: you may notice that most of the pronouns in this book are male. This was a decision made by my editors and me in order to keep the copy simple and consistent. It in no way means that that this book is more applicable to boys or that I intended the tips and advice in this book to be just for boys. So, if you happen to have a daughter (like I do), please mentally substitute "her" for "him" and "she" for "he" as you read. And then write a very serious letter to whoever invented the English language, letting them know how much easier our lives would be if pronouns weren't gender specific.

ONE

Getting into the Big-Kid-Mama Groove

Surviving and Thriving as You Transition into the Grade-School Years

It's a little bit ironic that the first time (ever) that Joey slept past 6:00 a.m. was on his first day of kindergarten.

During Joey's toddler and preschool years, I had literally tried every possible strategy to get Joey to sleep in. We begged. We pleaded. We bribed him with chocolate chip pancakes on any day that he slept past seven. Which never happened. We even got one of those "Okay to Wake" clocks that glowed when it was okay for him to get up, which only resulted in him waking me up at 5:00 a.m. to check and see "if the clock was still working." It was.

Anyway, by the time Joey turned five, I had given up on

turning him into a late sleeper. We made a rule that he had to stay in bed—reading or whatnot—until the sun came up. If he wanted to wake up at o'dark thirty and just lie there, then that was his prerogative. And so he did, morning after morning, month after month, year after year. Until that hot day in August when he had to go to school for the first time. On that day, he decided to sleep in. In fact, I had to drag him out of bed by 6:30 to make sure we made it to school on time.

The next day, he slept in again.

And on that Saturday morning, he slept until eight. Eight in the morning! And as he trudged down the stairs in all his bedheaded glory, he announced to me that now that he was in kindergarten, he was going to start sleeping like a teenager. (Because, in case you're wondering, teenagers sleep until eight. Or something like that.)

I hate to be the one to break the news to you, but your kid is growing up. And that means your parenting is going to have to grow up a bit too. You probably no longer have to worry that your kid is going to wake up at 4:42 a.m. and dump Cheerios all over your bed. Or have a potty accident at playgroup. Or have a meltdown in the middle of the Target aisle. (Unless, of course, a sugar-low coincides with a sale on sticker books, in which case all bets are off.)

Big-kid parenting is just different from baby or toddler parenting. Where before you were vigilant, now you have to be strategic. And where before you were black-and-white, now you can start to add some color to your parenting. You can add some orange ideas here and a bright turquoise discipline choice there. And before long, you'll discover a whole rainbow of possibilities with your big kid. Okay, enough with the cheesy metaphors—I'm sure you get it. Your kid is bigger. And that means you have to start parenting bigger too. I've written this book to help you do exactly that. But first, here are a few tricks and tips to help you get into the big-kid-mama groove.

How to Get into the Big-Kid-Mama Groove

1. Think before you act.

Back in your toddler-mama days, you had to think fast. Because if you didn't make a diving leap in front of your kid as he walked toward the mud puddle, he was certainly going to find a way to get every drop of water from that puddle into some place that it didn't belong. But now your kid is a big kid. And with that comes a measure of security. You probably don't have to worry that he's going to touch the hot coals in the fireplace or smear sweet potato puree onto the underside of the couch cushions. And that security buys you time to think a bit before you act. Nothing is as pressing as it was when your kid was small.

So what exactly does more-thinking, less-reacting parenting look like? It means instead of jumping to reprimand or reward your kid, you spend some time thinking about the best way to approach each situation. And—even more important—you allow your kid to spend time contemplating the best approach to each and every situation as well. So instead of jumping to your kid's rescue when he's struggling to figure out how to put together his Legos, allow him the space to ask for help. And when he misbehaves, don't intervene immediately, but allow both of you some time to cool off and consider things. Because the more you allow yourself—and your kid—to think, the more he's going to learn and grow.

2. Lean on God more than ever.

Letting go is hard. Remember that story I told you in the introduction about the day I dropped Joey off at kindergarten for the first time? What I didn't tell you is that after I pulled out of that parking lot, I had to pull my car over because I was crying so hard that I couldn't see. I sat there on the side of the road—within view of the school—and sobbed for a good twenty minutes. Because my baby took my heart with him as he walked into that school.

My motherly instinct is to hold on—to cling to my children as if they are mine to hold and protect. And while I know that God's purposes for my children require independence, my mother's heart still needs some convincing. Because when my eyes see big kids—kids who are ready to face the big, wide world and all that comes with it—my heart still sees those tiny, precious babies I once cradled in my arms. Tiny babies who have grown up way too fast.

I know I still have a lot more letting go to do—I can't even imagine the tears I will shed when my tiny babies move on to middle school and then high school and—I don't even want to think about it—college. But now, while each tiny step feels like a rite of passage of its own, I'm learning to lean on Christ more than I ever have before. I cannot fulfill my job as a mother by clinging to my own understanding—because my human emotions and desires stand in the way of God's bigger picture. And only by turning to Christ will I teach my children that they, too, can turn to Him as they grow.

3. Rely on prayer.

I'm a fixer. If I could, I'd like to pave the road for my kids with rainbows and cotton balls so that if they ever hit a snag, they'll land on a cuddly cloud of softness. (I'm sure Joey will love it when I talk like that when he's a teenager. Especially in front of his friends.) Anyway, when Joey mentioned to me one day last year that a kid in his class—let's call him Mr. Meanie Pants—had called him a "wimp" at school and refused to play with him at recess, I wanted to call up Mr. Meanie Pants' mom and tell her exactly what I thought of her kid's bully tactics. That'd teach him to mess with my kid.

But I didn't call because I knew that part of growing up is learning to do things on your own. Well, that and I didn't have Mr. Meanie Pants' mom's phone number. Instead, I prayed. I prayed that God would give Joey the insight to stand up for what is right. I prayed that Joey would learn how to discern right from wrong on the playground without becoming a bully or a victim. I prayed that I would know the words to say to help him learn important attributes, like courage and kindness and respect.

I honestly don't know what happened with Mr. Meanie Pants. I have a feeling that by the time they hit the playground on the next day, both kids had probably forgotten about the incident and had moved on. Because Joey never mentioned Mr. Meany Pants again in a negative light.

I have to say that the incident with Mr. Meany Pants taught me a valuable lesson. (And no, it wasn't that playground politics should be left on the playground, although that's important too.) I learned that while my mama-bear instincts might tell me to toss gumdrops and lollipops at my kids, to make sure their days are happy, my Christian instinct should always be to turn toward prayer. Because while I won't always be able to fix things for my kids, I can always rely on God to stand in the gap for them.

4. Make quality time a priority.

Once your kid starts school, those easy-breezy days when you had nothing to do but sit around in your pajamas and read the same stories over and over and over are, well, over. And I'm telling you this because I know how much people love it when I state the obvious. But also because I want to save you the embarrassment that will certainly come when your kid shows up at school and tells his teacher that he spent his summer eating Cap'n Crunch out of the box because "mommy didn't have time to wash the spoons."

Schooling takes time—and whether you send your kid to school or homeschool, the amount of free time you have to just hang out with your kid will certainly decrease. But I'm a quality over quantity type of person. I mean, think about it: would you rather have a whole bag of M&M's or one really amazing piece of rich, expensive dark chocolate? Okay, forget that analogy, because the obvious answer is both. But my point is that even if you don't have a ton of time with your kid, you can still make that time count.

One thing I do is set aside after-school snack time as "us" time. I whip up a from-scratch batch of chocolate chip cookies—okay, I feed him Goldfish crackers—and spend a half hour talking to him about his day. I also try to do something fun as a family each weekend—go on a bike ride or go bowling—so there is something nonschool and non-chore related that we can do together at least once every week. Whatever we're doing, I make it a point to spend quality time with my kids every day.

Ready, Set, Invest

Throughout this book I hope to give you tips, ideas, and strategies to go beyond simply parenting your kids. Because I know that's simply not enough. Instead, I want to help you invest in your kids' Christian heritage—not their future success, their academic achievement, or that football scholarship you're hoping for—but in who your kids are in Christ. Because the truth is, as you send your kid out into the big, wide world, your ultimate goal is not that your kid will learn to stand on her own two feet, but instead, to learn to stand on the Rock.

. . . .

Time-Out for Mom

For When You're Preparing Your Heart to
Send Your Kids Out into the World

"Know therefore that the Lord your God is God; he is the faithful God, keeping his covenant of love to a thousand generations of those who love him and keep his commandments." (Deuteronomy 7:9)

Heavenly Father, I am so grateful for Your faithfulness! I know that You have a covenant of love with Your children, and that is such a comfort to me! I am scared right now, Lord. I am getting ready to send my baby away from the shelter of my nest and into the world.

Guide my words and my actions, Lord, so I can prepare my child to be a servant, a disciple, and a follower of You. Help him shine bright in a dark world so Your love will be evident through everything he does. Amen.

. . . .

10 Things to Remember as You Send Your Kid Off into the Big, Wide World

1. There's a reason that glitter glue and baby wipes were on your school supply list. And it's the same reason that you shouldn't send your kid to school in the eighty-dollar suit that your mother-in-law got him for Easter.
2. Make your kid memorize the following: *I will bring my lunch box home from school every day.* Because there's a hard-and-fast rule at my house that mommy doesn't pick moldy carrot sticks out of the cracks of lunch boxes.
3. Your kid may say he understands the book checkout system in the library. He may even *think* he understands the book checkout system in the library. But you should probably go over it again before the next class library day. Because twenty confused kids equals one frustrated librarian and the chance that your kid won't be able to check out the new Fly Guy book until next week.
4. "Because I said so" *is* a perfectly acceptable answer to the question, "Why can't I bring my pet lizard to school?" But that doesn't mean your big kid won't try to find out why exactly it's such a bad idea for himself.
5. The desire to be clean apparently must develop post–elementary school. So that battle you've been doing to get your kid to bathe, well, it will continue for the foreseeable future.
6. It's still okay to kiss your kid good-bye. Just do it quickly, before his friends see.

7. Even if your kid can read to himself now, he will still love it when you read him a bedtime story.

8. Just because you pack kale chips and a sprouted hummus sandwich in your kid's lunch, doesn't mean he's going to eat them. Chances are—smarty pants that he is—he'll find a way to swindle the girl next to him out of her Twinkie by saying that his quinoa bake is "a princess pie."

9. Your kid is watching you. And that means that your little meltdown over the fact that daddy is coming home late *again* will not only be stored in his little brain under "appropriate ways to react when frustrated," but will also probably be reported in full detail to his teacher, friends, and guidance counselor tomorrow.

10. Your kid may be a big kid, but he still needs his mommy. Make room for those gangly legs on your lap, and give your kid the time and space just to be with you. Because no kid is ever too big for mommy snuggles. Except for maybe a teenager.

TWO

The Fifteen Factors

*Doing What It Takes to
Help Your Kid Succeed*

've never actually seen or tried a magic potion, but I imagine that if I did, I'd really like it. Imagine how simple life would be if you could take a swig of some chocolate-covered-cherry delight and your stress instantly disappeared. A gulp of peach-cinnamon smoothie and that pile of laundry on your bed is folded. A sip of sparkling lemonade and suddenly you and your husband are whisked back to your honeymoon phase (and you'd still be able to pull off that hot-pink bra you bought way back when—I'd plunk down a good five hundred bucks for a bottle of that).

But I'd trade a lifetime supply of all of the aforementioned potions to get a bottle of Success-Guaranteed Juice for my kids. I imagine it would be some rainbow, sparkling, chocolate chip concoction that the kids would guzzle every day when they came home from school. And that concoction would guarantee that my kids would not only be successful in school—but also in life. In their walks with God. In their relationships with people. In their financial and work-related endeavors. What mom wouldn't want that?

Alas, there is no such potion. But the good news is that we as Christians have something better—God's perfect love for our kids. One guarantee we have as Christians is that God loves us (and our kids) in a way that surpasses all understanding. Which means God is working behind the scenes to bring His perfect plan into fruition—a plan that is exactly perfect for each and every one of our kids.

You see how I just used the word *perfect* three times in one paragraph? That wasn't an editing mistake (or my inability to use a thesaurus), but simply my effort to explain to you that God's plan is—you guessed it—perfect. Which means we can trust that our kids are in *His* hands and that *He* has a plan. And His plan is better than any magic potion for success.

Now that I've reassured you that God is in control, I want to remind you that God has called us to be active participants in the stewardship of our kids. Which means you can't just sit around sipping magic lattes while waiting for God to act. Instead, we imperfect parents are called to team up with our perfect God to lay the foundation for success for our kids. But before we go any further, I have a little confession to make: I don't really know what I'm doing. I can't give been-there-done-that advice because I simply haven't been there or done that. My oldest kid is six. He has never won the Nobel Peace Prize or led a team onto the mission field. He has yet to ace a spelling test. He was wearing diapers fewer than four years ago, for goodness' sake! And so, with this in mind, I feel very inadequate standing here telling you what you need to do to help your kids succeed in school and in life. I'm just a mom—a mom with young kids and a busy schedule, who is just trying to figure it all out as I go.

But I have discovered a magic potion, if you will, and that miracle is my mom, Ellen Schuknecht. I consider her a master educator and parenting expert—not only because she raised such an amazingly hip daughter (ha!) but because she has more than thirty-five years of experience working as an educator and parenting advocate. She was an early childhood teacher for more than fifteen years before she became an elementary school principal, leading two large elementary campuses to academic success. Now she works as the family ministries coordinator at a Christian school where she counsels parents and teachers on how to help their children succeed. Kind of makes you want to hire her to come live next door and help you raise your kids, doesn't it?

Well, what you have in your hands is the next-best thing, because I strong-armed my mom into helping me write this book. (Helpful hint: the best way to bribe Grandma into doing something is to guarantee her time with her grandkids.) I've taken all her best been-there-done-that advice, insights, and ideas for raising successful kids and included them in sections throughout, titled "From the Principal's Office." What's more, I've spent a lot of time consulting with my mom on every chapter of this book to ensure that the information I'm giving you is not only accurate, but that it actually works.

Above all, my heart in writing this book isn't to tell you what to do and how to do it, but to walk with you on this road and to share my own journey with you. Because when we walk together—as Christian mamas, friends, and sisters in Christ—we can learn together. And raise amazing, God-loving kids in the process.

Defining Success

When I talk about raising successful kids, I want to make it very clear that I'm not talking about worldly success. Because, as nice as it would be if your kid grew up to be a surgeon (or a fairy, which is my daughter's current dream career), academic achievement is simply not what's most important to God. Now, I know I'm walking down a slippery slope here, because I understand we live in a world where success matters. I also know we live in a world where our ability to function in society is contingent upon our ability to work and use our minds—the minds that God gave us to use. And because of this, I want my kids to achieve in school. I want them to learn to read and write and think for themselves. And I'll admit I *do* want them to get good grades. I beam every time I see an A—or a smiley face, which is the equivalent of an A in kindergartenland—on my son's work.

But I'm learning that true success is much more than that. God wants your kids to love Him passionately with every ounce of their beings. He wants them to love mercifully, to trust wholly, to hope undoubtingly. And as we send our kids off into a world where academic and material success are applauded, we have to teach our kids to reach for more. To reach toward the God who created it all and to hope for something bigger than the world can offer. To hope for Him.

I think the first step to guiding your child toward true success is to realize that there's a big difference between how the world defines success and how God defines success. And that's why when I refer to *success* throughout this book, I won't be talking about your kid getting a full-ride scholarship or landing a job making $1.3 million a year. What I will be talking about is God's definition of success, which is so much more than money or power or fame. Because God's definition of success is a heart that seeks Him. And more than anything, that's what I want for my kids.

. . . .

Time-Out for Mom

For When You're Considering Your Kid's Success

"Each of you should use whatever gift you have received to serve others, as faithful stewards of God's grace in its various forms." (1 Peter 4:10)

"Blessed is the man
Who walks not in the counsel of the ungodly,
    Nor stands in the path of sinners,
    Nor sits in the seat of the scornful;
But his delight *is* in the law of the LORD,
    And in His law he meditates day and night.
He shall be like a tree
    Planted by the rivers of water,
    That brings forth its fruit in its season,
    Whose leaf also shall not wither;
And whatever he does shall prosper." (Psalm 1:1–3 NKJV)

Almighty God, You have given my kids all the talents, abilities, and spiritual gifts they need to follow Your plan for their lives. Lord, help them use those gifts to serve You first and others second, so that Your will is accomplished in their lives. Lord, fill their lives with trusted teachers and advisers who can lead them toward You and Your promises. Help them turn to you as they learn and grow so they can lead fruitful and prosperous lives. Amen.

. . . .

The Fifteen Factors

I know I told you that there isn't a magic potion to guarantee success-ful kids—and there isn't—but what I didn't tell you was that I do have something that can help—The Fifteen Factors. After having parents ask again and again what it takes to raise successful kids, my mom started contemplating the shared characteristics of kids who man-age to thrive academically, socially, and spiritually. Through years of observation and contemplation, my mom narrowed her list down to fifteen characteristics—a list that I have affectionately named The Fifteen Factors. This list doesn't guarantee success for your kids, but instead gives you something you can reference, work toward, pray over, and nurture in your kids in hopes of giving them the tools they need to succeed.

A few years ago my mom started focusing on growing these fifteen specific attributes in the students in her school, and she found that instilling these factors in her students helped them grow strong foundations for genuine, lasting faith—and academic and social success followed. (To this day, she continues to write practical tips and ideas on how to apply The Fifteen Factors on her blog, familywings.org.)

Because of my mom's success in applying this list of principles to her students' lives, I've decided to use these principles to shape the principles in this book. Of course, I'll talk about lots of other things—but my main goal in this book is to help you take The Fifteen Factors and make them consumable for your kid so that you, in turn, can send your kid off into the world with the tools he or she needs to be successful. Without further ado, here is the list.

. . . .

The Fifteen Factors

1. Genuine faith: A faith that is personal and real.
2. Vision: A long-term hope that aspires to follow God's plan.
3. Resiliency: The ability to bounce back from setbacks and failures.
4. Wise decision making: A willingness to make good choices even when it's not easy.
5. Work ethic: The understanding that effort, more than talent, produces success.
6. Responsibility: A choice not to make excuses or cast blame when there is an issue.
7. Courage: A willingness to try in spite of fear of failure.
8. Focus: The ability to concentrate on a given task.
9. Godly knowledge: A strong foundation of biblical understanding that leads to a sense of what's really true. (Truth=God, by the way.)

10. Self-control: The ability to delay gratification in order to do the right thing.
11. Discernment: The capacity to distinguish good and evil, right and wrong, reality from fantasy.
12. Self-motivation: The desire to work toward a goal without extrinsic reinforcement.
13. Teachable spirit: A humble spirit that's willing to listen and learn.
14. Honesty: The willingness to tell the truth even when it means admitting to a mistake.
15. Positive attitude: The choice to try rather than give up; to be thankful instead of grumbling; to encourage rather than complain.

Nurturing The Fifteen Factors

Just in case you haven't quite gotten the point of the last several pages (in which case you may need to go grab yourself one of those magic lattes), I'll summarize: The Fifteen Factors is a list of characteristics that lead to *true* success—not just worldly success but also successful relationships and most important, a true and lasting faith in God. And by helping our kids to attain and internalize these characteristics, we can help them succeed in school and in life.

It sounds simple, but I know what you're probably thinking: *How exactly can I nurture The Fifteen Factors in my kids?* Unfortunately, there's no easy answer for that, but I am going to try (with a lot of help from my mom) to give you tools and ideas throughout this book that can help your children grow and thrive. That said, here are a few ideas to get you started:

1. Pray for and encourage the God-given factors your kid already has.

Close your eyes for a moment. Wait—you can't close your eyes while you're reading, so open them back up. Spend a few moments thinking about your kid. Think about the many ways God has gifted your kid. Did God give him a knack for understanding people's feelings? An uncanny ability to sing just like the VeggieTales guys (only louder)? The ability to whip up a stunning cheese soufflé and Gorgonzola salad while you sit back with your feet up, waiting for him to serve you on a silver-plated tray? Yeah, mine wasn't gifted with that one either.

God gave your kid a plethora of talents and abilities. And if you look at your kid's natural abilities and compare them to The Fifteen Factors, you'll probably see some parallels. For example, my son Joey is fearless—he'll ride any roller coaster or jump off the top of any playground slide. This manifests itself not only in semi-regular trips to the emergency room, but also in courage—at school he is willing to try new things and learn new skills. Likewise, my daughter, Kate, is one of those kids who will practice things again and again. She'll spend hours drawing one picture just to make sure it's absolutely perfect. And when she's in school, this shows up as a work ethic that's willing to try and try again even when things are hard.

I'm guessing that you can probably see two or three or maybe even four characteristics on The Fifteen Factors list that your kid is really good at. Your child may naturally possess discernment or responsibility or (if you're really lucky) self-control. And these factors can be considered your "bonus" factors—things your kid just naturally *gets*. But just because your kid is naturally adept at these factors doesn't mean you can automatically check them off the list. Instead, use these bonus factors as building blocks upon which to help your child develop all the other factors. Pray that your kid will use his natural sense of *courage* to grow *self-control*. Encourage your kid's natural *discernment,* and tell him that you hope it leads to *godly knowledge.* Help your kid grow a *work ethic* through his God-given *positive attitude.*

2. Set "heart goals" instead of "head goals."

Not to steal a quote from your high school debate coach, but if you don't have goals, you're never going to reach them. Same goes for your parenting. Everything you work on and pray for should be with a long-term vision in mind. (And we're going to talk a lot more about having a vision in chapter 4.) I want to encourage you to make a shift in your goal setting from "head goals"—goals that simply focus on worldly success—to "heart goals"—goals that help your kid's heart move toward God. Here are some examples:

Head Goals	Heart Goals
I want to get good grades so I can go to college and earn a lot of money.	I want to learn to work hard in any situation so God can use me as He sees fit.
I want to be a great writer/athlete/actress/scientist.	I want to use my God-given abilities to bless others.
I want people to respect me.	I want to love and honor God with everything I do.
I want to be a good friend.	I want to learn to serve others selflessly.
I want to win the award.	I want God to get the glory for the acts I do on earth.

3. Talk (nonchalantly) about the Factors.

You can go ahead and trust me that telling your kid to start using her discernment will probably result in nothing but a blank stare. I know. I've tried it. But I want to encourage you to make The Fifteen Factors part of the daily vocabulary you use with your child. For example, when your kid works really hard to complete an assignment, say to her, "Wow! I can see your work ethic is really growing!" Or when your kid decides (just once) not to hit his sister when she snatches his toy, mention offhandedly that he showed self-control in making that decision.

Put The Fifteen Factors on Your Fridge

Now I have a job for you. It's pretty easy, as long as you remembered to pick up printer ink last time you were at Staples. Ready? Go to my website, www.christianmamasguide.com, and click on "Freebies." On that page, you'll find a printable PDF copy of The Fifteen Factors. Print it out. Laminate it if you want. And post it on your fridge (in a spot that's high enough to protect it from grubby fingers using it as a doodle pad).

The reason I'm having you put The Fifteen Factors on your fridge is because I want it to be the thing you see when you go to your fridge each morning to get the creamer for your coffee (or the wheatgrass for your smoothie, if you're that type of girl). Because this is your kid's must-do list, to help him become the person God intented him to be.

THREE

The Most Important Factor

Helping Your Kid Find a Genuine Faith

et's take a little journey back to 1996. Back to a time when boot-cut Gap jeans were making their debut and Tom Cruise in *Jerry Maguire* was all we needed to feel complete. Back to a time when the "Macarena" was cool, Coke Zero hadn't been invented, and only the superrich had cell phones (and even then, those cell phones came in black vinyl briefcases). Back to Mariah Carey on the radio and *Friends* on TV and . . . oh, sorry; I got distracted by my nostalgic trip back in time. Back to my point: I started college in 1996.

And as I moved out on my own for the first time, I admit that there was a smidgen of rebellion in me that was just waiting to break away from my middle-class, Christian upbringing. I had always been the good girl. In high school, my biggest rebellion was probably wearing pink socks with a blue shirt. And I only did that once. But as I moved away from the safety of my home and my parents, I started to reconsider everything I had ever believed. It's not that I ever stopped believing in God—I didn't—but for a while, I stopped believing that the things I did really mattered to Him. And with that shift in my beliefs, I started testing the boundaries of my faith. I stopped going to church. I experimented with alcohol. I started to believe that the fun of now mattered more than the hope of the future. And that shift rocked my faith to the core.

After my existential faith crisis of 1996, I lived on the edge of faith for several years. I knew in my heart that God existed, but I refused to take the time out of my life to make Him the basis for how I lived my life. And so I trudged on—living a life that clearly wasn't going anywhere, clinging tenuously to what I hoped my future would hold while despairingly looking at who I had become and wondering what had happened to the sparkling faith I'd held as a child. Those were sad years. And had God not intervened, I'm not sure how long I would've walked forward with a hard-on-the-outside, mushy-on-the-inside, half-baked faith.

But God did intervene—in Costa Rica, on September 11, 2001, of all dates. My new husband and I had reached a rock-bottom point and literally picked up what was left of our fragile dreams and moved to Costa Rica for a few months. It may sound like a glamorous newlywed adventure, but it was more like a try-to-find-odd-jobs-while-living-off-rice-and-beans type of adventure. And when we woke up to the news of the terror attacks on our country on September 11, we were not only shocked and scared and saddened, but also desperate. Desperate for the solace and peace that would only come from the God we no longer knew.

Wandering on a dirty public beach that morning, we stumbled upon a prayer rally. It was led by an amazing missionary couple, Linda and Lewie Richie from Tia Linda Ministries, who later took us into their home and fed us, both spiritually and physically. A few weeks later we flew back to the States, broke and jobless, but for the first time in our short marriage, not hopeless.

I wish I could say that things have been easy breezy ever since, but life never works that way. I can say that over those next few years, God drew us into His arms—resulting in us eventually joining our lovely church and community group here in Austin. And through God's intervention in my heart, as well as the prayers of warriors like my mom, my dad, and my grandma, I am once again walking with God. But it took a long time—years, really. And I don't want that for my kids.

Why is it that so many kids like me—from Christian homes and strong backgrounds—get lost in a sea of lukewarm faith and convenient Christianity? And—more important—how can we as parents raise our kids to go out into the world with a faith that thrives? A faith that hopes in Christ? A faith that loves without fear? A faith that chooses what's right instead of what's easy?

The first factor—a genuine faith—is the most important of The Fifteen Factors. Hands down. The rest of the factors can be intertwined, mixed and matched, prioritized here and there, but a genuine faith is always number one because, without it, your kid simply cannot be successful in life. Sure, he can earn money or get a job or get married, but without genuine faith, your kid will never live the life that God intended for him. And while you can't wrap up genuine faith in a pretty package and give it to your kid for Christmas, you can point him to the One who can give him the tools he needs to make his faith real. Then your kid can go out into the world—first in kindergarten and later in middle school, high school, and college—with a rock-solid faith that won't slide when faced with an ungodly culture (and things like the "Macarena").

Who Can We Blame?

In this crazy, narcissistic culture where kids have cell phones before they are two and iPads before they are eight, it's no wonder kids are falling away from their faith in droves. And it's not as if the other kids are helping! I mean, there are first graders out there who have—get this—older siblings who teach them about faith-crushing things like (gluttony-inducing) fruit snacks and (non-Christian-music-promoting) Spotify. It's a mess out there.

Clearly, I jest. Because as parents, we can't blame the world for our kid's faith—or lack thereof. Sure, it's a messy world. There are all sorts of things out there that I would like nothing more than to protect my kids from—forever. But recently, I've done a lot of thinking and praying and talking to people who know a lot more than I do about this issue, and I've come to a conclusion: It's not what our kids are learning and hearing and doing out in the world that's hurting their faith, but instead what they are *not* learning. It is how they are *not* growing that is making them wither. And it is what we are *not* teaching them that's causing them to stray from their faith in Christ.

I have to admit that when I first started thinking about helping my kids grow a genuine faith, it felt a bit overwhelming. I'll remind you again what I've had to remind myself over and over: there is no magic potion guarantee for our kids' faith—and that's terrifying to any Christian mama. But let me remind you of this also: Your kid's faith isn't up to you. It's up to your kid and God. The Bible tells us that we are each given a measure of faith—a gift (Romans 12:3; Ephesians 2:8–9). *(Thank you, God!)* This gift is not based on works. *(Thank you, God!)*

While you do have a role to play in the nurturing and growing of your kid's faith, it's ultimately not up to you. Philippians 2:12–13 says, "Work out your salvation with fear and trembling; for it is God who works in you both to will and to do for His good pleasure" (NKJV). That's Bible-speak for: Your kid's faith is up to your kid and God. So while you can (and should) be an active participant in the development of your child's faith—a mentor and a teacher—ultimately, you have to put your kid's heart, soul, and mind into God's hands. (Which, by the way, is the place where he or she is safest anyway.)

What I said may be (slightly) unpopular with some of you because it puts a lot of pressure on you as a parent while simultaneously taking away all the control you have. But hear me out. God—the

One who is unchangeable—created us to grow and change more and more into His likeness throughout our entire lives. Growth and change are invigorating. In fact, growth fuels more growth. The same is true in the reverse. When our kids don't grow, they become complacent. One way or the other, they are moving in some direction. And so, to help prepare and nurture our kids so they can have a strong, unshakable faith, we need to nurture them to grow in Christ each and every day.

Nurturing faith in preschoolers is easy—well, *easier*. Young kids soak up stories about Noah and Moses and Jonah and the whale like little sponges. They learn songs and say prayers and learn all of the "Christianese" they need to garner a robust "now-that's-a-good-girl" response from adults. But big kids start asking the real questions. And thinking about God in a way that goes beyond a Bible story here and a worship song there. And that's when true growth toward a genuine faith begins.

I'm still in a place that's halfway between "Pharaoh-Pharaoh!" and "Why does God love us?" with my kids. And right now, my greatest prayer as a mom is that my kids will internalize everything they're learning about God. That they will grow and learn and change into the men and women God wants them to be. Because in twenty years, I don't really care if my kids have good jobs or fancy cars or nice spouses. (Okay, I sort of care. It'd be fun to borrow their BMWs and take them for a spin.) My most earnest wish for my kids is that they leave my home and enter the world with a genuine, unwavering faith.

. . . .

Time-Out for Mom

For When You're Praying for Your Kid's Faith

"Jesus answered, 'I did tell you, but you do not believe. The works I do in my Father's name testify about me, but you do not believe because you are not my sheep. My sheep listen to my voice; I know them, and they follow me. I give them eternal life, and they shall never perish; no one will snatch them out of my hand. My Father, who has given them to me, is greater than all; no one can snatch them out of my Father's hand. I and the Father are one.'" (John 10:25–30)

Eternal Father, I want my kids to be Your sheep! Lord, You have made it clear to each and every person on earth that there is power and grace associated with Your name. And now, soften my kids' hearts so that they, too, will know You wholly. Hold them tight, so that nothing and no one can ever pull them away from Your love. You are the only one who can save them, and I hand their precious souls to you. Hold them tight, God. Amen.

. . . .

From the Principal's Office

What Does the Bible Say About Growing Genuine Faith?
by Ellen Schuknecht

I'll let you in on a little secret: you already have the ultimate resource for growing a genuine faith in your kid. In fact, it's probably sitting on your coffee table or on your nightstand right now, just waiting for you to pick it up and start using it. And no, I'm not talking about that glass of water that you keep forgetting to bring to the dishwasher. I'm talking about the Bible. (But you already knew that, didn't you?) Whenever parents ask me for a book to help them foster a genuine faith in their kids, I always point them first and foremost to the Bible. The Bible (naturally) is chock-full of helpful tips and ideas. Such as:

1. Unlike your own words, the Word of God is alive and active. God's words have the supernatural power to invade and capture hearts and minds, so integrate God's words—straight from Scripture—into the words you say. (Hebrews 4:12)

2. The Bible is sufficient for *all things* you encounter in life! So

get in the habit of seeking His wisdom first—and encourage your kids to do the same. (2 Timothy 3:16–17)

3. Hide God's Word in your heart (*and* in your kids' hearts) by memorizing Scripture together—so that in times of struggle and confusion, you can draw on "stored" truth to steady yourselves. (Deuteronomy 11:18)

4. Model prioritizing "whatever is true, whatever is noble, whatever is right, whatever is pure, whatever is lovely, whatever is admirable" in your life so there won't be room for the opposite: deception, depravity, and ugliness. (Philippians 4:8)

5. Make time in your family's schedule for God. Go to church regularly. Pray together. Serve those in need as a family. (Romans 14)

6. There is nothing your kids can do to earn God's love. When you converse with your kids—and especially when you discipline your kids—focus on what Jesus accomplished for them so they can be encouraged by their hope in Him instead of discouraged by their own struggles. (Ephesians 2:8)

7. Teach your kids to listen for God's voice as they walk through life. It's hard to develop a habit of listening to God—most adults struggle with this—but God's voice leads to Spirit-led choices, which, in turn, lead to eternal life in Christ. (Galatians 6:8)

8. God's standards do not change regardless of circumstances; lovingly and consistently hold your kids to the standards you establish. (Psalm 119)

9. Model prayer as your first and primary action in dealing with any circumstance. (1 Thessalonians 5:16–18)

. . . .

How Have "Older" Moms Grown Genuine Faith in Their Kids?

Now, I'm not calling anyone old per se, but some of my friends are, well, older moms than me. I have no clue how old they actually are (for all I know, they're twenty-three), but I do know they have kids who are old enough to do things like read their Bibles without help sounding out the words or go to youth group without a chaperone. Which means that these moms have been doing the motherhood thing for much longer than I have—and therefore probably have some great tips about how to make faith real in kids.

6 "Old Mom" Tips to Help Grow Faith in Your Kids

1. Openly and appropriately share your own mistakes with your kids. My children know that I was boy-crazy in my teen years and that I didn't focus on God nearly as much as I did on any male that walked by me. I explain to them that this resulted in my learning to put human relationships over God—something I struggled with for years. Then I talk to them about what I learned from my own mistakes so that, hopefully, they won't have to learn the hard way, as I did. —*Christina Berry Tarabochia, mom of five*

2. Encourage your kids to be servants from an early age. Show them that they can always do something—pray for a friend, turn off the lights, carry something to the table, be kind when no one else is being kind—to share God's love with others, and in turn to feel God's love themselves. —*Leslie Montgomery, mom of two adult kids and two younger kids*

3. We have a box of "Scripture cards" that we keep inside our silverware drawer. At dinner hour, everyone chooses one card and reads the Bible verse on his or her card. Then, over dinner, we discuss the meaning of the verse and how we can apply it to our lives. We started this when our youngest was six—and she could hardly read the big words on the cards—and now that she's fourteen, this tradition has not only become a great and meaningful family activity, but also a way to help our kids internalize their faith at the same time. —*Cynthia Herron, mom of one adult kid and one teenager*

4. I started a prayer journal with my fourth-grade daughter.

We sit together every night and spend time together lifting up the issues that are important to her in prayer. At first, she prayed for the "things on her list"—new toys, friends at school—but as she's grown in her prayer life, she's started praying for truly deep and meaningful issues—the poor, the lost, the lonely. Recently she prayed for our government! It's amazing to see how her prayers have grown and also how she has grown in the process. —*Susan DiMickele, mom of three middle school–aged kids*

5. It's not about what you do. It's about what you *don't* do. When you answer every want and need, they'll never learn to lean on Jesus. Parents become God to their children when they do their chores, help with their homework, protect them from losing, and rescue them from every uncomfortable situation. To instill faith in our kids means we have to place their hope in God instead of us. —*Joanne Kraft, mom of four teenage and adult kids*

6. Make the most of little moments, like in the car on the way to and from school or when your kid is just falling asleep. For me, God always seemed to come up when we were outside playing. I would show them the bugs and flowers and marvel at how God made all that for us, and the questions would just come. Kids have no problem accepting that God is there 24/7, and can so easily live in the moment of that comfort and trust. I think that's what Jesus meant in saying that we needed to come to Him as children. It's living in a constant awareness of God's presence and expecting Him to show up. Kids get that. It's a no-brainer for them. —*Dineen Miller, mom of two adult daughters*

Back to the Detour

Back to me, back to me. Remember that faith detour I told you about in the opening lines of this chapter? The years where I stepped away from the God I knew from my childhood and the faith my parents had assumed was solid? I'm sure it killed my parents. In fact, I bet when they read this chapter, they'll probably start wondering and worrying about all the things they could've and should've done to help me solidify my faith as a kid.

I don't want to sound like a cheesy dating show, but the truth is that it wasn't them; it was me. I had a rebellious spirit. And I let the world influence me. But even during the worst times, there was a part of me that desired God. And the faith training I had as a kid—as well as the foundation of Scripture I knew and the prayers of my parents and grandparents—eventually created in me a desire to run back into the arms of the God I had always loved. Same goes for your kid. There is nothing you can do to assure his or her salvation. But you can lay the foundation so that on his darkest days, he'll know where to turn to find the light.

FOUR

Catching the Vision

*Stepping Forward with a
Christ-Centered Vision*

There was a time in my life when I had a dream to be a famous track star. Now, those of you who know me (and know of my adamant dislike of anything sweaty) are probably laughing right now at the mere thought of me attempting to compete in a track meet. But there was a time when I was actually pretty good. Well, *good* is a relative term. There was a time when I had no problem running around the track—multiple times—without feeling as if I wanted to hurl.

So as track season approached during my freshman year of high school, I got ready. I signed up for the team. I checked out my uniforms. I even convinced my mom to loan me the money to buy a new pair of Nike Air running shoes—the kind with neon orange laces. It was the '90s, people! Neon was the ultimate cool, meaning that I was going to be the ultimate cool on the track team.

To say I was ready would be an understatement. Those new shoes were virtually burning holes in the track by the time

I stepped onto the field that first day of practice. I was itching to run—to feel the wind behind my back, the thrill of victory. (Or, the thrill of at least finishing.) But coach had different ideas. Because while I wanted to run, he wanted to talk. He pulled out a big piece of poster board and a package of Sharpies and wrote in huge letters across the top of the board, "This Season." Then he asked us to map out our vision for the season.

The whole vision thing really threw me for a loop. Goals, I'd done those thousands of times—little did my coach know that he was going to have an Olympian on his hands soon—but vision? My coach didn't care about us winning the state championship (okay, he cared, but not at that moment) or about us reaching individual goals. Instead he wanted us to think about the character traits—hard work, perseverance, courage—we would develop through the season. He wanted us to catch a vision for what track would do for us as people.

Since this was back before I realized how much I hate running, it really motivated me. Not to run faster, but to run with courage. With persistence. With a vision for my future in mind. And that's how we should be thinking about this new season in our kids' lives as well. It's easy to get them ready for school—well, as easy as a trip to Target on tax-free weekend can be—but it's hard to get them *ready* for school.

As we send our kids out into the big, wide world, many of us send them off unprepared. Not unprepared materially or socially or even academically, but unprepared to understand the vision God has for their lives. And that unpreparedness hinders their ability to grow into the people God intends for them to be. So I'm ready to be your coach—to bust out the poster board and the Sharpies and help you to find the vision for your kid's first school year so he can walk into the world confidently and prepared to learn and grow.

I talked about your kid's need for Jesus in his heart, mind, and soul in regard to discipline in *The Christian Mama's Guide to Parenting a Toddler*. Because the truth is that regardless of your parenting style or your kid's personality, your kid needs Jesus in order to thrive. And now, as you're sending your kid off into the big, wide world, this concept has all sorts of new ramifications. Because you're sending your kid off into a big, wide world that also needs Jesus. Desperately. And I don't mean to freak you out—at least not too much—but there's a lot of nasty stuff out in that world.

Now, before you go shutter your windows and start researching grocery delivery services so you don't ever have to leave the house again, let me tell you something else: God has given your kid all the tools he needs to not only survive, but to thrive out in the big, wide world. And with some coaching from you—dry-erase board and all—your kid will be able to catch the vision for who exactly God wants him to be and what he'll need to do to get there.

The Need for a Vision Statement

I have to confess that when my mom suggested I write a family vision statement before Joey started school, I immediately dismissed the idea. Honestly, it felt like a very pseudo-inspirational thing to do. And since I'm really not into things like Hallmark movies or pictures of kittens dressed like babies, I figured I could just skip the whole vision statement thing and move on to more important things, like, say, teaching my son to read.

But after a few months of kindergarten, I started to sense a shift in Joey. He was doing great in school—academically—but he was coming home emotionally drained, exhausted, and seemingly frazzled. It was as if he poured all his energy into his school day and yet came home feeling defeated, as if his work and effort didn't have a purpose. And I started to realize that my mom may actually have known what she was talking about.

The thing is, having a vision for your kid doesn't have to be some warm-fuzzy statement that you cross-stitch onto a sampler and hang on your wall next to your kitty photos. It doesn't even have to be written down. But by coming up with a vision for your kid and for your family—a dream of where you want to go in the next ten years—you create an anchor for your kids. You give them something to hang on to so they can say, "This is me, this is who I am, and this is who I want to be . . ." And that, my friends, is why Vision is the second of The Fifteen Factors.

My inner teacher is trying to burst out a bunch of edu-speak on you right now—because this is a concept that teachers learn early on in college when they're studying how kids learn. The concept of giving your kid an anchor is called "scaffolding." And it's a strategy that teachers use all the time to help kids learn. Basically, you can't just throw information at kids in isolation—a math fact here, a phonic sound there. Instead, you have to give them a framework with which to organize information in their heads. So the math fact has to connect to the bigger framework of numbers, which connects to the real-life applications for math.

Anyway, I'm getting way too deep into teacher talk right now, but my point is this: You have to give your kids a framework with which to organize all the information that is pouring into them at school. And while the academics will be scaffolded by their teachers (or you), their vision for who they are has to be scaffolded by you and God. By giving them a vision statement—in essence, a glimpse of the people they want to become—you're giving them a framework on which to hang the messages they hear in the big, wide world. For example, when someone tells your son about a friend who needs help, he'll immediately refer to his vision—his scaffolding—and think, *Yes! I should help him because God desires me to be a person who serves Him by serving others.* Likewise, when a friend suggests that your daughter cheat on a test so she doesn't have to study, your kid will have a vision for herself that rejects that—because she has a vision that reminds her that she is an honest person.

This is obviously not black-and-white—your kid is still going to mess up even with a vision—but by creating a vision for your kid, you're giving him a framework to stand on as he learns and grows. And that's an important tool to give him as he works toward becoming the person God wants him to be.

. . . .

Time-Out for Mom

For When You're Considering God's Vision for Your Kids' Lives

"For this very reason, make every effort to add to your faith goodness; and to goodness, knowledge; and to knowledge, self-control; and to self-control, perseverance; and to perseverance, godliness; and to godliness, mutual affection; and to mutual affection, love." (2 Peter 1:5–7)

"Trust in the LORD with all your heart
　　and lean not on your own understanding;
in all your ways submit to him,
　　and he will make your paths straight." (Proverbs 3:5–6)

"But the fruit of the Spirit is love, joy, peace, forbearance, kindness, goodness, faithfulness, gentleness and self-control. Against such things there is no law." (Galatians 5:22–23)

"I lift up my eyes to the mountains—
　　where does my help come from?
My help comes from the LORD,
　　the Maker of heaven and earth.

He will not let your foot slip—
　　he who watches over you will not slumber;
indeed, he who watches over Israel
　　will neither slumber nor sleep." (Psalm 121:1–4)

"We know that we have come to know him if we keep his commands. Whoever says, 'I know him,' but does not do what he commands is a liar, and the truth is not in that person. But if anyone obeys his word, love for God is truly made complete in them. This is how we know we are in him: Whoever claims to live in him must live as Jesus did." (1 John 2:3–6)

. . . .

How to Write a Vision Statement

The good news is that there is only one resource you need to write a vision statement: the Bible. There's no need to go to the library to check out a stack of books or to pore over articles about God's vision. You don't even need to ask Mr. Google. (He's not very reputable when it comes to God's vision anyway.) God made it really easy. The Bible makes it really clear what God desires from His children.

Of course, just because it's clear doesn't mean it's easy. In fact, it took me weeks to figure out what I wanted our vision statement to say. Not because God didn't make it clear in the Bible what He desired for my kids—but because I felt so inadequate (not to mention unworthy) after reading scriptures that referred to God's vision for my life. The deep, fundamental values God desires us to have as Christians aren't easy to embrace—in fact, they're downright hard. Because they stand in opposition to everything the world tells us. The world is screaming at us to earn more, do more, and be more, while God is telling us that our treasure is in heaven, that His grace is sufficient for us, and that He is making us more like Him.

After much reading (for ideas on where to start your study, see "Time-Out for Mom" in this chapter), I decided to focus my family's vision statement on 2 Peter 1:5–8:

For this very reason, make every effort to add to your faith goodness; and to goodness, knowledge; and to knowledge, self-control;
and to self-control, perseverance; and to perseverance, godliness;
and to godliness, mutual affection; and to mutual affection, love.
For if you possess these qualities in increasing measure, they will
keep you from being ineffective and unproductive in your knowledge of our Lord Jesus Christ.

From there—after much prayer and consideration, and using
the verse as a guide—Cameron and I wrote a vision statement for
our family. Here's what ours says:

The MacPherson Family Vision Statement

As our kids venture out into the big, wide world, we want our kids to:

- develop a genuine *faith* that comes from truly knowing God
- build *virtuous habits* that reflect God's nature and character
- grow in their *knowledge* of Christ so they can understand on
  a meaningful level what His purposes are in the world and in
  their lives
- gain a sense of *self-control* so that doing the right thing starts
  to feel natural and good
- learn to *persevere* through things that seem difficult
- crave *godliness* in their lives, even when it's unpopular
- understand that *prayer* is not only a powerful means of
  communication with God, but also opens our spirits up to
  understanding God's will
- make *courageous* choices that honor God
- become servants who truly desire to *love* others by helping
  them

Helping Kids Catch the Vision

I know what you're thinking. Or at least I have a pretty good idea based on what I would be thinking: *It's great to write a family vision statement. But my kid is* five. *And even though he's the smartest five-year-old I've ever met, he's not going to get this, even if I display it at the top of the stairs for him to look at every night before he goes to bed.*

Here's my answer: I get that. Joey's pretty smart, too—he has, after all, passed an entire year of kindergarten—but even if I read our family vision statement to him every night before bed, he probably still wouldn't be able to wrap his head around the implications. It's big-Christian stuff. And he's just not spiritually mature enough to internalize it. But here's the thing about our God: He has given us a gospel that is so simple that a child can understand it. And in a big, complex world where many things don't make sense, His truths are the one thing we can count on to be simple. So while your kid certainly won't be able to fully grasp your family vision statement as a five-year-old, he can grasp Christ's love and, in so doing, allow God to reveal Himself to him slowly.

But let me bring this conversation out of the clouds—I've been entirely too theoretical the last few pages, and if you're anything like me, you're probably craving some practical advice. Well, practical advice and a bag of Dove chocolates that you don't have to share. So here are some easy ways to make your family vision statement real to your kid:

1. Break it up.

One thing we did was choose a family vision theme for each month. For example, November was Brotherly Kindness Month at our house. And during Brotherly Kindness Month, we did all sorts of things to teach our kids about—you guessed it—brotherly kindness. The main thing we did was really have a lot of conversations surrounding what kindness is and what it means to love and serve others through our actions. We also made sticker charts for our kids.

We bribed (I mean, *encouraged through positive reinforcement*) our kids to be nice to one another by giving them a sticker every time we noticed a kindness. At the end of the month, each kid got a quarter for each sticker he or she earned, and with that money, each got to pick out a present for his or her sibling.

2. Have short but sweet conversations.

You say, "Our family mission statement is to improve this world through servant leadership, a passion for Christ, and genuine conversation (maybe over coffee and doughnuts) that lead to disciple-making relationships," and your kid hears, "It's my mission today to passionately eat doughnuts." Let's just say that if you would struggle to sit through a thirty-minute sermon on a family mission statement, your kid will probably struggle too. Even if you buy him doughnuts.

Perhaps a better approach is to weave your family vision statement into your daily conversations. So when you notice your kid working hard to finish a homework assignment, say, "Wow! I can see that you're showing perseverance, and that's one of the qualities our family has listed in our vision statement. Good job!" Or "I noticed you showed self-control by not hitting your sister when you were angry. I've been praying that God would show you how important self-control is to your character."

3. Pray about it.

Let's say your kid is having a hard time internalizing the idea that it shows a lack of self-control to smear glue in his sister's hair. And let's say that all your begging, pleading, lecturing, and preaching isn't doing much to help him develop self-control. Let me remind you: God moves through prayer. We moms want to do something—to fix our kids and their struggles—but sometimes (okay, oftentimes) it's enough to just pray. And using your family vision statement as a guide to pray for your kids is a great place to start.

Striving for Your Vision

This may come as a surprise to you, but I never ran in the Olympics. In fact, I didn't even make the Olympic trials. It turns out that those snazzy shoes—cool as they looked—weren't enough to make me a track star. Or even a mid-level track athlete. They were, however, enough to help me grow as a person. Because throughout that track season, I learned a lot.

I learned that, as painful as it is to run four miles (uphill) for training, it actually feels really good to know you accomplished something difficult. (Which, by the way, showed perseverance.) I learned that I can be just as invested in my teammates' success as I am in my own. Because, oftentimes, our friends have a lot of God-given talent to share. (Which taught me humility.) I learned that my plans and God's plans don't always align—for some reason, it wasn't in the cards for me to win the gold medal—but that His plans are always the best. (Which taught me to trust Him.)

And as I've reflected on my track experience (and dug around in my closet to try to find those shoes—I promise: neon is back in style), I've come to the conclusion that while my worldly vision for my kids may not come to fruition, the vision God has for them will. And all I have to do is keep my ears open so I can hear God's words and then guide my kids accordingly.

FIVE

Courage at the Great Divide

*The Place Where Stepping
Forward Means Stepping Back*

You have reached the great divide of parenting.

You've been trekking toward this place for the last five years, give or take. You trekked your way through months and months of sleep deprivation as your baby slowly figured out night (when it's dark) is for sleeping. You trudged on, fueled by chubby-armed hugs and leftover mac and cheese, through toddler tantrums and Mommy and Me classes and even that period of time when your kid decided that his one goal in life was to make sure the dog's water dish was always empty. You hiked up metaphorical mountains—fighting up the inclines to make sure you reached the top with your marriage, your kid, and your favorite pair of knee-high boots intact. And now our metaphor—oh, and your life—has finally come to the place you've been working toward: your kid is old enough to start school. And that kid—the one you've carried step after step for the last five years, is ready to step off your shoulders and start hiking on his own. Oh, wait; I said the metaphor was ending . . . but you get where I'm going with this, right? It's time for you to start letting go.

Just last week I had one of my more-stellar mom moments at the park. There was this big jungle gym–type structure on the playground that was clearly designed for professional athletes. The structure rose 482 feet (or at least 8) off the ground, and from what I could see from my angle, the bars looked slippery and the dirt underneath was rock hard. Oh, and there were big kids—like, second graders—hanging out on top. And my kids, who are not professional athletes or skilled acrobats, wanted to go up too. Naturally, I gave them my firm and entirely rational response: "No way. Never, ever, ever. Try it when you're twenty-six and living on your own."

But they persisted. Apparently, all of their friends were way up there at the top of the skyscraper of a jungle gym. And I was the only mean and nasty mom who had said no. So I took a deep breath and told them to go ahead. Then I hovered underneath, nonchalantly holding out my arms so I'd be ready to catch them if they fell. Which, by the way, they didn't.

I'm not sure if the altitude affected them, or if they just liked the chance to practice their dangling-precariously-over-bone-breaking-rocks skills, but they had so much fun way up there at the top of that jungle gym that they talked about it for days. And if I do say so myself, my laid-back, letting-go mama ways gave them a means by which to grow courage, to learn, to explore, and to gain confidence. Go me!

Letting go is hard for us moms. Those mama-bear claws come out at the mere thought of our kids getting hurt—physically, emotionally, or spiritually. And that makes it hard to even imagine letting our kids venture off into the big, wide world without us there to protect them. That, and you just don't know what your kid could be exposed to out in the world. For example, your kid could:

- gain an undying affection for something (or someone) called Bieber . . . whatever that is
- somehow get the idea that kids need cell phones ("for safety reasons") and figure out how to articulate said reasons to your husband
- find out that it's not really against the law to serve chicken nuggets without broccoli
- find out that it is, however, against the law to pee in public
- discover that it technically doesn't take that long to make pancakes for breakfast on a school day, because Billy Joe's mom does it, and she even has time to put her makeup on before going to school

And the list goes on. It's enough to make me consider strapping my kids to their bunk beds and never letting them out. (Don't worry; if I ever were forced to do that, I'd break my no-food-upstairs rule and serve them dinner on a tray, bedside.) And I'm not the only one. I polled my friends, and it turns out letting go of our precious, cherished children is the hardest thing we mamas have to do. Harder than sleepless nights. Harder than nonstop get-into-everything days. Harder than that time your kid found a bottle of shaving cream and mistakenly thought it was frosting.

Sending your kid off to start learning and growing on his own is a big step. You've been walking uphill toward this goal for years—teaching him, preparing him, nurturing him with endless hugs, kisses, and from-scratch PB&J sandwiches. And now it's time. Time for him to put those problem-solving skills (and those mad coloring skills) that you've so patiently taught him to good use.

You've reached the great divide.

Over the next few years, your kid is going to grow in all sorts of Fifteen Factors: resilience, wise decision making, responsibility, godly knowledge, discernment, and self-motivation, to name a few. But first you have to let go of him enough to let him start walking down the hill on his own.

Time-Out for Mom

For When You're Struggling to Let Go

"The LORD appeared to us in the past, saying, 'I have loved you with an everlasting love; I have drawn you with unfailing kindness.'" (Jeremiah 31:3)

"But he gives us more grace. That is why Scripture says: 'God opposes the proud but shows favor to the humble.' Submit yourselves, then, to God. Resist the devil, and he will flee from you. Come near to God and he will come near to you." (James 4:6–8)

Lord, You love my kids more than even I do! I am so comforted by that fact—because as I slowly let them go off on their own, I know that their heavenly Father is walking alongside them with an unfailing kindness and a love that surpasses any human love. God, give me humility to know that in order for my kids to grow and thrive, I must shrink. You are what matters. Draw close to me, Lord God, and draw near to my kids so that each of us may know You more. Amen.

Why Let Go?

Did you know that 100 percent of successful, Christian adults were once kids? And every single one of those adults once had a mother? And the vast majority of those mothers had a hard time letting go and sending their kids out into the world? But they did. And look where their kids are now: adulthood. Yep. The stats don't lie. If you let go, your kid will probably grow up to be an adult. Or something like that.

And if my clearly well-researched stats aren't enough to convince you (I have no idea why they wouldn't be), then let me pull out the big gun: the Bible makes it very clear that our children are not our own. Instead, they are unique individuals created for a purpose. And as parents, our job is not to shelter our kids from the world, but instead to send them out into the world to fulfill their God-given purpose.

Some of you reading this are probably feeling pretty smug right now, because if you've chosen to homeschool or send your kids to a Christian school, you may think you've found a way around this whole letting-go thing. And you're partially right—by choosing to homeschool or sending your kids to a Christian school, you do, in some ways, buy your kid a slower descent into the big, wide world. I'll get more into that in chapter 6, where I talk about school choice. But I'll tell you this right now: you're not off the hook when it comes to letting go. Because while "letting go" can mean many different things, God calls all parents to equip their children to step out into the world—to stand alone and learn what a life in Christ truly means. For some, that means sending their kids off to school with the tools they need to be evangelists and disciples in a dark world. For others, it means homeschooling while giving kids leeway to explore and think critically about essential theological concepts. Regardless, every single parent must let go of his or her kids so that they can figure out who they are and who they want to become.

And, not to be Miss Debbie Downer on you, but if you don't let go—well, then you're setting your kid up for a lot of disappointments. Because most colleges aren't going to let you move in with your kid and hold his hand while he deals with that "mean economics professor." There's going to come a point in his life where there's no one to help him make the ramen on the hot plate "just the way he likes it," and the sooner you start letting go, the sooner he's going to start learning his own ramen-making skills.

In Proverbs 22:6, God tell us to "start children off on the way they should go, and even when they are old they will not turn from it." You've done that. You gave your kid all the hugs, back rubs,

Bible stories, and Go-Gurt yogurt packs he needed to thrive as a preschooler. But now he's school age, and you have to trust that all the time and energy you've poured into that precious little heart will now carry him through those first few steps out into the world. It's kind of sad, isn't it? But it's also exciting. Because now is the time when your kid will really learn who he is and who he wants to be.

One final dose of encouragement: My mom told me that by letting our kids step out into the world on their own, we are actually holding on to what is precious about our kids. Because God loves your kid with an everlasting love and has great plans for his future. And only by letting your kid explore those plans on his own are you giving him—cheesy analogy alert!—the wings he needs to fly for Christ.

Reasons Letting Go May Not Be Such a Bad Thing After All

1. It turns out that the whole living vicariously thing isn't all it's cracked up to be. Especially when a successful day to your kid means building the tallest Lego tower ever.

2. With all the time you've saved now that you've stopped hovering, you may just have time to start working out. Or at least start thinking about working out.

3. It's about time you swapped out your trusty diaper bag for a mom bag. Winnie the Pooh doesn't go with your mom jeans anyway.

4. Considering the colored-pencil incident of last week, it's probably best if you distance yourself from your kid's book report.

5. After your performance during craft time at MOPS last week, it's becoming more and more apparent that you need a hobby.

6. This may be just the thing to convince your husband to let you have another baby.

How to Let Go

So let's say (hypothetically) that all of this talk about sending your kids out to be warriors for Christ (well, that and the fact that your kid is getting a bit too heavy to carry) has finally convinced you it's time to start letting go. But what exactly does letting go look like?

Fortunately, for moms like me (who at times still feel the need to ask their kids if they wiped well after going to the bathroom), letting go is a long, drawn-out process. And while you're not going to be sending your kid off with a microwave and a sleeping bag to live in an inner-city apartment on his own for a few years, it is now time to start letting your kid take a few steps away from you. Like onto the back patio, for example. And as you start the process, you're going to have to swap out some of your old preschool-mom habits for new, grade-school-mom habits. Here are some tips:

1. Replace talking with listening.

Last winter, on the night before school was going to start again after Christmas break, Joey burst into tears as I was tucking him in. I figured he was nervous about going back to school, so I started chattering away about all the great fun he was going to have back at school. He'd get a new library book. And new reading partners. And get to tell his teacher all about what he did over the break. And how there was really no reason to be nervous, because he loved school and loved his teacher, and it was going to be great.

But as I chattered on and on and on, I noticed that his tears kept falling. Unsure of what to do to help him, I finally climbed into bed and rubbed his back, and we sat there in silence for almost five minutes. And then I heard a quiet voice from under the covers: "Mommy, what if my friends all forgot who I am?" I was dumbstruck. I thought he was nervous about academics. And he just wanted to make sure he still had his friends.

Unfounded as his worries were—trust me; no one could forget

Joey—he was genuinely scared of what was going to happen. And I had gone on and on about his nervousness about going back to school without taking the time to find out what was truly bothering him. Rookie mom mistake, eh?

Big kids need a listening ear more than a jabbering mouth. And I'm trying—unsuccessfully at times—to remember to shut my mouth and listen before I start going on and on and on. Because now that my kids are articulate enough to express what's going on in those little heads, I need to give them the space to do exactly that.

2. Replace telling with modeling.

"Wow, Joey! What a great picture!" I said as my obviously proud five-year-old showed me his latest masterpiece as he hopped into the car after kindergarten one day.

"It's a picture of you and daddy. Mr. C. told us to tell him about something that our mommy and daddy like to do. So I drew you guys in the shower."

"Um, in the shower?"

"Yes, I told him that you guys like to take showers together every single day."

Isn't that fun? Now, let me make one thing clear to every person who reads this: these showers that Joey talks about are entirely and completely practical. At least most of the time. We have three kids and a busy schedule, and we happen to also have a big walk-in shower in our master bedroom. So, for time and convenience (yes, 100 percent time and convenience), we occasionally (okay, frequently) take showers together.

Joey's lovely picture—which for some reason I forgot to hang on the fridge—serves as a reminder to me that my kids are watching every move I make. (Well, that and that I should probably lock our bathroom door when I'm in the shower.) Because I have three pairs of eyes that are watching everything I do. And three sets of ears that are hearing every word I say. And three little minds that are learning who they are and where they come from by observing who I am.

Now, I don't want to cause you to freak out when you think about the way you acted last week after your husband made that comment about the unmopped floor, but let me just say that your kids saw everything you did in response. They noticed those deep breaths you took while you tried to think of a response that didn't involve you throwing a wet mop at your husband. They noticed the way your emotions shifted from hurt to frustrated to downright angry. They even noticed when you passive-aggressively explained to your husband that perhaps it was time he learned to use a mop. They saw it all.

Now I'm going to throw some psych-talk at you. And this isn't coming from the perspective of a psychologist—something I'm clearly not—but instead from that of a parent. As your kids reach their grade school years, they're going to start realizing that they have their own choices to make. And the way they learn to respond to those choices will be heavily influenced by what you've shown them. Not what you've *told* them—what you've *shown* them.

3. Replace answers with questions.

My daughter, Kate, is the exact opposite of Joey when it comes to sharing her feelings. She's like me—she vomits her feelings out the second she feels them, so I never have to worry whether she's sad or angry or double-super-chocolate excited with a cherry on top. Because she'll tell me. And so, when I'm talking to her, it's tempting to gush on and on about how fantastical any given topic is without stopping to think about the fact that she is old enough to (a) form opinions of her own, and (b) use those opinions to shape her viewpoints of the world.

I'm learning to ask questions.

Why did that make you sad?

How can you best handle that anger?

What can we do to help other people feel happy like we do?

And, not surprisingly, those questions have led to deeper, more meaningful conversations with Kate. Because instead of me telling her how she should feel and why she should feel it, she's been forced to wrap her mind around her own responses—which, by the way, has helped her grow in discernment and wise-decision making.

4. Replace watching with trusting.

There's just something about a preschooler that trains moms to be utterly untrusting. Take my one-year-old, Will, for example. He is absolutely untrustworthy. Just the other night, he dumped four boxes of cereal, a box of raisins, and a container of coffee onto my pantry floor in the 7.9 seconds it took me to grab a head of lettuce and some carrots out of the fridge. Or maybe I lost track of time. Either way, I've been adequately trained to keep my eye on him at all times.

But my big kids? I highly doubt either of them is going to dump piles of food onto the floor. (Unless it involves some bizarre science experiment fathomed by their mad-scientist uncle, Troy, in which case, all bets are off.) Therefore, my big kids can be trusted. For the most part. And yet I've been so trained by years of forced watchfulness that sometimes I keep my nonstop eye on them as if they are babies.

I'm breaking this habit. In fact, just the other day, my big kids wanted to go outside and play on the swing set by themselves. While I stayed inside and fed the baby. I wanted to say no. To tell them they couldn't go outside where they could get hurt or get into a fight or get into trouble. But I took a deep breath and said, "Sure! I trust you guys to do the right thing!" And they were so proud.

. . . .

From the Principal's Office

Helicopter Mom Syndrome
by Ellen Schuknecht

I think most moms are helicopter moms in one way or another. I know I was at times when my kids were younger. It stems from the worthiest of ideals: we love our kids and desperately want to ensure their happiness and success. So we hover. And we swoop in when we sense trouble. And we do everything in our power to make sure our kids don't taste the bitterness of defeat or struggle. Unfortunately, I've seen time and time again that hovering helicopter moms accomplish just the opposite. Having mom standing by to whisk them away from any semblance of trouble doesn't create a barrier of protection in kids, but instead creates a sense of codependence that adversely affects kids as they're learning to grow resiliency, wise decision making, responsibility, and self-control (which are all characteristics in The Fifteen Factors). And none of us want that.

So how can we as moms stay involved, in tune, and communicative with our kids without becoming helicopter moms? Here are some of my tips:

8 Ways to Avoid Being a Helicopter Mom

1. Instead of jumping forward as supermom-saves-the-day when your kid reports a problem at school, listen and offer suggestions. This communicates your belief in her ability to handle difficulties and solve her own problems.
2. When your kid struggles, be a coach, a cheerleader, or even a model—but don't ever do it for him. Sure, you could solve that math problem correctly with your eyes closed. But getting the right answer is rarely the point.
3. Expect responsibility. It's obviously faster when you pack your kid's backpack for him—and you certainly won't forget his reading homework on the counter *again*—but learning what it takes to keep himself organized and ready is a skill that many kids don't have. And it will serve him well both in school and in the future.
4. Don't immediately pick up the phone to call the teacher or coach or school when your kid is upset. Go to God first in prayer. If,

after twenty-four hours, he's still upset, then proceed with open and honest communication.

5. Don't make rash judgments based on what you hear from your kid. Another side to the story almost always exists and—shockingly—kids are experts in sharing what serves them well and leaving out what does not. Listen carefully, but never take action without considering that there is probably more to the story than what you're hearing.

6. Erase "it's not fair" from your vocabulary. And from your kid's. Life is often not fair. Tsunamis are not fair. It's not fair that pop stars make more money in one year than your entire school of teachers. Teach him that it is more important that no one suffers from *his* injustice than for him to look for and always expect what he considers justice from others.

7. It's (sometimes) good when your kid fails. Feeling regretful about a bad grade or a poor choice is a great motivator to help him grow. So let your kid experience the pain of disappointment and figure out what is needed to do better next time.

8. Likewise, never blame others for your kid's disappointments. Statements like "You were robbed of the medal" or "You deserved better" or "Your project should've won the science fair" do much more harm than good. Even if they're true.

The View from the Other Side

Do you remember that analogy I had about the great divide? About how you trek uphill to get your kids to the point where they can start walking on their own? And since I've told you that you've now reached a place where you can start trekking down the other side, you can assume that the rest of your years as a mom will be a slow, smooth downhill coast, right? Unfortunately, this is where my analogy falls apart.

Because letting your kids go certainly doesn't mean you are

done being a mom. In fact—just the opposite. Those bumps and pitfalls on the trail can really impact your kid. And since your kid is walking on his own, you may not see them until he has already fallen down. And that's why in the upcoming chapters, I'm going to talk to you about how you can use these steps to choose the right school for your kid, how to prepare him to go to that school, and how to grow the Fifteen Factors in the process.

SIX

Choosing a School

*Sending Your Kid off to
the Right Place*

I send my kids to public school.

And just by saying that, I've immediately caused half of you to feel relieved (Yes!—someone else to talk to about the evils of cafeteria mystery meat and gym class), while the other half of you are already formulating an e-mail explaining to me what exactly goes on inside public schools. Because your cousin's best friend's aunt once told you that, well, let's just say it can get pretty nasty out there.

I'm going to take a stand right here and right now: there is no right choice when it comes to school choice. There. I said it. Public school, private school, homeschool, classical school, Montessori school, flipped school, online school, and un-school are all right for some families. Honestly, I kind of wish there was one right choice. Like if I knew that every single student who graduated from a Christian classical school automatically got accepted into a top university and then unfailingly went on to get a great job and join a great church while living the perfect Christian life, well then you'd better believe I'd be sending my kids to a Christian classical school. The choice would be easy!

But unfortunately for us moms who stress over decisions like this, there is no 100 percent tried-and-true, right answer. Don't believe me? I asked Mr. Google. And—surprisingly—he was pretty ambivalent about which type of school was best. In fact, he told me that research has shown that there is little indication that school type alone really affects future success. Or affects a kid choosing to follow Christ. Lots of successful Christian adults went to public school. Plenty were homeschooled. Some went private. Some went Montessori. But none of these methods—or any of the others—has proven to be a definite factor in future success.

What Mr. Google (and my mom) *did* tell me is that while there is no one right choice for *all* kids, there is probably a right choice for *your* kid. Because God created a unique learner with a unique personality when He created your little one—and that unique personality will most likely be honed best in a certain setting. And so your job is to prayerfully consider your options so you can send your kid off into the big, wide world in the best way possible. And I'm going to help you do that. Well, me and God. Not necessarily in that order.

. . . .

Time-Out for Mom

For When You're Praying About School Choice

"He who did not spare his own Son, but gave him up for us all—how will he not also, along with him, graciously give us all things?" (Romans 8:32)

Lord God, there are so many choices when it comes to school! And right now I'm at a loss as to where my kid will be best educated, but also where he will best serve You. But Lord, You've spared

nothing when it comes to generously filling our lives with everything
we need. And I know You will continue to do so as we decide which
school is best for our kids. Lord, I pray You will reveal Your will to me.
Graciously show me where my kid will learn and thrive—and where
his precious spirit will be protected and nourished. I hand this deci-
sion over to You—because You know me and my child better than we
know ourselves. Amen.

. . . .

Choosing a School

School choice is stressful.

And aside from deciding on Joey's name (after much delibera-
tion, we decided that Danger really couldn't be his middle name),
and my decision to finally allow him to eat a peanut butter sandwich, choosing a school was one of the most stressful parenting
decisions I've made thus far. In fact, the sheer stress of making a
choice that helped Joey have a positive, nurturing, and successful
school experience drove me to the unthinkable: Microsoft Excel.

Okay, I admit it wasn't a complicated spreadsheet, with formulas
or anything, but I did create two columns (I made the headers bold
all by myself, *thankyouverymuch*), and I wrote down the four school
choices available to us in our area: public school, private school,
the university model school, and homeschool. And I deliberated for
hours over the pros and cons of each choice.

I have the distinct disadvantage of having family members and
friends working for each of the aforementioned institutions. My
husband is a public school assistant principal. My mom is the family
ministries director at the university model school. My dad is dean
of students at a private Christian school. Oh, and many of my best
friends homeschool. So I have access to lots of information about
each school type. (Wait; did I say disadvantage? I meant *advantage.*
I mean, who doesn't love having a million different people telling
you a million different opinions nonstop for days?)

All that to say, making a school choice was hard for me. And—I hate to do this to you after you built your spreadsheet and everything—I learned there simply isn't a four-step process to doing it right. And I'm guessing that even the most meticulous spreadsheeters probably still struggle to find an obvious choice. That said, I do have some tips to make your decision a bit easier. Here's what helped me:

1. Pray first. And last.

The only person who knows undoubtedly which school choice is best for your kid is God. (It has to do with that whole omniscient thing.) And so I encourage you to sprinkle—okay, shower—every conversation, every bit of research, and every decision you make with prayer.

2. Try to keep an open mind.

I actually didn't *want* to choose public school for my kids. The idea of sending my kids off to a school where they could have non-Christian teachers and non-Christian friends was terrifying to me. And so, when I started considering schools, I wanted to leave public school entirely off my little spreadsheet. But after some prayer and consideration, God changed my heart and made it pretty clear that public school was the direction in which He wanted us to head.

3. Ask your friends.

Find out where your trusted friends send their kids to school. One of my friends discovered this amazing little homeschool co-op in our community that has worked great for her—and while I ended up not choosing it for my kids, it's nice to know I have other people out there who are doing the same research and discovering options I may not have heard of. Plus, by asking around, you can get some great inside information—class size, the price of uniforms, the fact that you have to hike two miles uphill in the rain to pick up your kid from school every day—about whatever schools you're considering.

4. Don't listen to anyone else.

I know I just told you to ask around—and that's a great thing when researching—but try not to get caught up in other people's opinions when it comes to school choice. School choice is a hot topic (see "The Courtroom of School Choice" at the end of this chapter), and people have lots of opinions. But their opinions—passionate and heartfelt as they may be—do not take into account what you know about your kid. So pray and form your own opinions, and take everyone else's words with a heaping tablespoon of salt.

5. Remember that no decision is permanent.

There is no law that requires you to leave your kid in the school you choose for her. Yes, that's right. If you start out sending your kid to that fancy-schmancy private school down the road, only to find out that the fancy-schmancy private school down the road teaches more diva skills than reading skills, you can move your kid. Easily. This is not a permanent decision. Unless, of course, you decide to tattoo your kid's school name on her wrist, in which case it will take some laser treatments before you make the switch. Either way, you're not signing your kid up for a lifetime of public school or homeschool or private school just because that's what you choose for her in kindergarten.

School Types

There are a million (okay, at least a hundred) types of schools out there, so there is no way I can give you information on all of them. That's what Mr. Google and your handy-dandy spreadsheet are for. I can, however, give you some basic information about the pros and cons of some of the most common school choices for Christian parents. Here's what my research and experience (that and the chit chat at my MOPS table) have taught me:

Public School

As I said, I chose public school for my kids. What I didn't tell you is that this was a very, very difficult decision for us. There are naturally tons of pros to public schools (have I mentioned that there are no tuition bills?), but there are also some pretty significant cons. (And if you're dying to find out exactly why public schools are so great, and yet not-so-great, I wrote a handy pros-and-cons chart at the end of each section, summarizing the pros and cons of each school choice. Feel free to skip ahead.)

Sending your kid off to public school is like sending your kid into a poker game. You just don't know what cards your kid is going to get. The teacher is a wild card. The students are a wild card. What your kid gets for hot lunch on any given day is definitely a wild card. And now that I've managed to turn your kid's education into a high-risk gambling game, I'm sure you're just itching to call up your local school district and sign your kid up.

Let me start over: there are many wild-card factors when sending your kid off to a public school. There are some amazing public schools out there. And there are even more amazing public school teachers. And amazing kids go to these schools. Your kid has the potential to get a great education, have a phenomenal teacher, and make great friends in a public school. But—and here's where you really have to get in tight with Mr. Google—there are also some pretty darn awful public schools. And not-so-great teachers. And kids who know the lyrics to "First, Second, Third, Elementary Nerd" and aren't afraid to teach your kid the song. And while you can't control all of these wild cards, you certainly can do your research to make sure that your local public school meets your standards.

My husband was actually the driving factor for us in choosing public school. He's a public school administrator and feels pretty strongly that Christian families and Christian kids need to invest in the public school system. He also feels strongly that only by allowing our kids to be exposed to different points of view can we give them the tools to be disciples in the world. And while my immediate reaction to that idea was that *other* people's kids could be exposed to different points of view and *other* people's kids could be disciples in the world, I did eventually come around to see that by prayerfully and purposefully sending my kids into the world—a world that I can't fully control—I am allowing God to work in their hearts and grow them into the people He intends them to be.

The Pros and Cons of Public Schools

Pros	Cons
It's free.	"Free" doesn't exempt you from that whopping tax bill you pay every time you buy a pair of jeans. Oh, and the "required" school fund-raisers.
You can be certain your kid's teacher went to school to be a teacher. (Because it would be bad news if they let an astrophysicist try to teach your kindergartner.)	You cannot guarantee that your kid's teacher will teach Christian values. In fact, many public teachers are required to teach concepts that are far from it.
Your kid will get access to cool programs and classes, like art, music, foreign language, soccer, and dance, all at no additional cost.	There are still costs such as that $200 pay-to-play fee, $50 to chip in for the coach's gift, and $180 in uniform fees.
The cafeteria makes lunch for your kid. Buh-bye, Jif and jelly.	Dino-nuggets and Jell-O aren't generally recommended as a healthy lunch. Of course, if your kid picks the "fresh veggie" option, that will up the health factor. Operative word: *IF*.
Your kid gets the chance to share his Christian values with the non-Christian world.	The non-Christian kids get the chance to share their values with your kid.
Your kid will have access to expensive services (think: special education) that you would otherwise have to pay for.	You don't get to choose the people delivering special services (think: special education)to your kid.

Private Christian Schools

The main reason we steered away from sending our kids to a private Christian school was money. We simply couldn't afford the tuition at the top private school in our area. But, oh, if we could have . . . Joey would have had access to incredible facilities, amazing resources, and godly, dedicated, and well-trained Christian teachers. And don't even get me started on the uniforms. A kindergartener in a school uniform may be among the most adorable things ever.

Anyway, I was definitely intrigued by the amazing opportunities there are for kids at private Christian schools. As a general rule, these schools hire teachers who have signed a statement of faith, so you know your kid is being educated by people who value the same things you do. Plus, since private schools usually have fancy things, like endowments and grants and educational funds, they typically have all sorts of snazzy things, like technology, lab equipment, and organic, homemade, hot-lunch programs. It's the Cadillac with a silver fish sticker on the bumper of the educational system.

There are, of course, other cons to a private education (listed below in chart format to make it really simple), but for many people, the positives far outweigh the negatives. I also want to point out that there are ways to pay the tuition: there are all kinds of scholarships and grants available to families who want to send their kids to private schools, so if you feel God calling you to go to a private school and money is the only thing that's stopping you, then I encourage you to look for other funding sources before entirely discounting the option.

The Pros and Cons of Private Christian Schools

Pros	Cons
Your kid is around Christians. Which means his friends, his mentors, his teachers, and his coaches will all share, and hopefully encourage, the same values you do.	Just because it's a Christian school doesn't mean everybody acts perfect. Christian kids—and Christian teachers, parents, and administrators—have real-world problems and face real issues just like anyone else.

Pros	Cons
Your kid will have access to state-of-the-art facilities, technology, and equipment as she learns.	Yes, there are *three* zeros on that tuition statement. And that doesn't include the supply fee.
The teachers are not only dedicated, but they pray with your kids, and share Scripture and study God's Word with your kids.	Your kid is rarely (if ever) exposed to other viewpoints—which means he's rarely (if ever) given the chance to stick up for what he believes.
Logic. Biblical History. Rhetoric. I bet you've never heard of classes like that in a public school.	Who really understands logic class anyway? I'm kidding! I totally understand logic. I think.

Homeschooling

I love the idea of homeschooling. In theory, at least. Just close your eyes for a second and imagine with me: Your kid wakes up without an alarm (so at 5:46) and comes down to your bedroom to snuggle. As you wake up, you read from the Bible together. Then you go make breakfast, after which you head to your in-homeschool room and start to work. Together you work through English and math and science; then, after lunch, you head to the state history museum and study social studies together. It sounds downright dreamy.

But I know myself, and I know my kid, and I know that my days would turn out nothing like the aforementioned dream. Because— this may surprise you a little—I tend to be a bit high-strung. And my kid—well, let's just say when we work together, we clash like a peanut-butter-and-cheddar-cheese sandwich. And I have a feeling that my attempts at homeschooling would end up like my attempts at dancing. Which means I'd fumble around with long division for a while before realizing that I was never in a billion years cut out to be a math teacher. Or a homeschool mom.

Anyway, homeschooling isn't for me—not because I don't think it's an amazing thing to do (it is), but simply because I firmly believe that if you're going to homeschool, you have to do it right. And I'm not cut out to do it right. I don't have the patience or educational savvy or ability to calmly watch while my kids blow up baking soda volcanoes on my newly mopped floors.

But some moms do. My friend Kelly homeschools her kids, and I'll tell you this: they are getting the most amazing education ever. They do tons of things they would never get to do in a public (or even private) school, and what's more, they get to do it all from the comfort of their home. With their mom as a teacher.

The Pros and Cons of Homeschool

Pros	Cons
Your kid gets to stay home with you all the time.	Your kid gets to stay home with you all the time.
You get to learn all sorts of fun things with your kid: music, art, and how to make a volcano out of Popsicle sticks and baking soda.	Your kids gets to learn all sorts of fun things at home: music, art, and how to make a volcano out of popsicle sticks and baking soda.
You never have to leave the comfort of your home—even on a rainy day.	Your living room becomes the gym on rainy days—and as you well know, dodgeball *is* part of gym class.
You don't have to pay tuition fees or fund-raising fees, and school lunch can consist of leftovers.	Just because you don't have to pay tuition doesn't mean you don't pay. Have you seen the price of homeschooling materials? Or supplies? Oh, and you probably deserve a salary as well.
Maybe this time you'll finally "get" long division.	The last thing you want to do is relive "that long division incident."

Parent Partnership Schools

I have to admit that, until a few years ago, I had never even heard of a parent partnership school. But now, "parent partnership" has become a buzzword akin to "Coke Zero" and "that new type of lunch box that has compartments." New parent partnership schools pop up every year. And more and more parents are trying to figure out exactly what they are and how they function.

Let me make it really easy on you: Think college. Without the dorms, the cafeteria, the professors, or the frat parties. And that helps you not at all. The gist of a parent partnership school is that students and parents get to choose the classes their kids take, and then the parents partner with the teachers through a mix of home-school and traditional school to provide schooling. So, for example, you could enroll your kid in math and English and then turn your dining room into a homeschool art studio and let your budding Monet study art at home. Or maybe reverse that and do the quiet, clean subjects at home. Either way, it's your choice.

When we were choosing a school for Joey, we strongly considered a local parent partnership school. I loved the idea of sending him to school two or three days a week and having him home the other two days. I also loved the idea that he could get a classical education with at-home components—times when I could learn with him and coach him. And I still would say that if I didn't send Joey to public school, my next choice would be parent partnership.

The Pros and Cons of Parent Partnership Schools

Pros	Cons
All the benefits of homeschool/ private school and un-school wrapped up into one happy place.	Yes, you have to (I mean, *get to*) deal with homeschool parents, private school teachers, and moms like me all in one supposedly happy place.
You can schedule classes to fit your schedule—which means you can keep your kid in soccer and ballet without missing school.	If you think your schedule is crazy now, you should try juggling a mix-and-match schedule of classes along with soccer and ballet.
All that stuff about private Christian schools—Christian teachers, Christian kids, Christian janitors—also applies to parent partnership schools.	All that stuff about your kids never being around anyone but Christians also applies.
You can homeschool your kid in Spanish and show off your mad Spanish skills.	Homeschooling isn't about showing off your own skills—mad as they may be. Your kid actually has to learn something.

Parent partnership schools are often less expensive than private schools. Which means your kid can get a private education without you having to take out a second (or third) mortgage.	There's less tuition because you're doing half of the work.
You get a built-in opportunity to get directly involved in your kid's education.	As the old proverb goes, too many teachers spoil the soup. Or something like that. But when two (or more) people are teaching the same coursework, there are bound to be moments of confusion.

· ·

From the Principal's Office

A Parent's Role in Each School
by Ellen Schuknecht

You have to be intricately involved in your kid's schooling. Don't get me wrong—the last thing your kid needs is someone to step in and micromanage his learning. (Which means you should probably step away from the glue stick and your kid's diorama.) But by taking an active role in your kid's schooling—regardless of which school type you choose for your child—you're showing your kid that his future matters to you. Plus, it also enables you to be aware of what's going on so you can be equipped to maintain your God-given role as the primary authority figure and shepherd in your kid's life.

That said, many parents aren't sure what their role is in their kid's education. And let me assure you, your roles are many: Cheerleader. Confidant. Tutor. Encourager. Friend. But these roles vary significantly depending on the type of school you choose. So, as you consider school choice, I want to outline the varying parent roles for each school choice so you can get a glimpse into how your role will be affected by the decision you make now.

School Options	Parent Roles
All Options	Model being a learner yourself.
	Be your child's secure anchor by maintaining a positive attitude through both the "ups and downs" that comes along with schooling.
	Refrain from negative discussions about the school or teachers in front of your children.
	Know what your kids are learning and connect it to their real lives when possible.
	Read with them daily.
	Limit TV.
	Coach and guide them to take responsibility and initiative as learners.
	Be on time both to drop off your child and pick him up.
Public School/Public Charter School	Check homework each and every night.
	Read every parent memo and notice.
	Be involved. Volunteer to help, if possible, in your child's classroom and with school events.
	Talk with your kids regularly about what is going on. Listen carefully and be attentive to signs of discouragement or depression, which can be the result of bullying.
	Get to know your child's teacher and his other viewpoints. Set yourself up to be your kid's most capable, wise, and loving authority; be who she comes to first with her questions about life.
	Purposefully and regularly provide what the public school cannot provide: spiritual training. Teach your child what it means to love the Lord with all her heart, soul, mind, and strength.
	Maintain a focus on the greater vision for your child. Nourish him daily with the living and active Word of God, and help him put God's words into memory so they are hidden in his heart as he goes about interacting with others in his school.
	Pray for your child daily. Go first to God with your concerns before going to others.

Private Traditional School	Check homework each and every night.
	Read every parent memo and notice.
	Be involved. Volunteer to help, if at all possible in your child's classroom and in school events.
	Talk with your kids regularly about what is going on. Listen carefully and be attentive to signs of discouragement or depression, which can be the result of bullying.
	Be informed and knowledgeable about the school's philosophy and worldview. Set yourself up to be your kids' most capable, wise, and loving authority; be who they come to first with their worldview questions.
	Don't assume a private Christian school or teacher can take your place in being the primary spiritual mentor for your child.
	Maintain a focus on the greater vision for each child by nourishing him or her daily with the living and active Word of God. If the school does not require Scripture memory work, set it up yourself so God's Word can be hidden in your kid's heart.
	Pray for your child daily. Go first to God with your concerns before going to others.
Homeschool	Do your research. Make sure you have high standards for reading fluency, reading comprehension, writing, and arithmetic.
	Don't make assumptions (high or low) about your child's level of achievement.
	Establish a yearly plan and develop an agenda each week that keeps you on pace to accomplish your goals.
	Be prepared in advance of each day. Establish a daily routine, and don't allow exceptions to become the norm.
	Include deadlines and timed assignments so your child learns the skills of time management.
	Don't multitask school time with your kids. Refrain from picking up the phone or computer, so you can be fully present when you teach.

	Connect with local organizations that support homeschooling families to avail yourself of the limitless resources available to homeschooling families.
	Pray for your child daily. Go first to God with your concerns before going to others.
University-Model Schools and Other Parent Partnership Models	Be fully informed as to what the various school expectations are for parents, and be willing to carry them out.
	Attend training sessions whenever possible, because the parental role in these schools requires active involvement in the educational process.
	Be prepared in advance of each day by knowing what the expectations for the school day at home are and what supplies you will need to carry out the activities. Make sure to read carefully all instructions sent home.
	Establish a daily routine, and don't allow exceptions to become the norm.
	Pray for your child daily. Go first to God with your concerns before going to others.

The Courtroom of School Choice

Even after careful and prayerful consideration for school choice, you may hear the occasional judgment about whatever school choice you make. Who am I kidding? You'll probably be barraged by at least four people a day (along with their mothers) about your school choice. I hear it all the time. In fact, just in the last few weeks, I've heard these total untruths come from the mouths of parents I know:

- ᕦ "If you don't give your child a classical education, he won't have the skills to succeed in college."
- ᕦ "Homeschool kids are so sheltered from the world that they automatically rebel when their parents finally give them some leeway."

∽ "I'd rather go into debt and make sure my child does well in school than send my kid to a free school where he won't get a decent education in anything except sex, drugs, and greed."

There's a lot of unnecessary hullaballoo over school choice. Especially in the Christian world. And it's kind of sad to me that instead of working together and trusting our fellow Christian mamas to make the best choices we can for our families, we're getting all judgmental. If you need something to judge, go to the gym and watch yourself in the mirror at Tae Bo. Or if you're a coordinated type, watch me. But don't judge other mamas for doing the best they can. And certainly don't judge them for making a different choice than you did.

You know your kid and your family better than that passive-aggressive lady at the park who told you oh-so-unsarcastically, "It's so great that you're sending your innocent children into the bowels of the public school system to be salt and light where there is so little salt and light." Ahem. Bowels of the public schools, my patootie. Ignore the judgers! Because when it comes to school choice, everyone has a different opinion. Make the best choice for you and your family, and then trust God to protect your precious kid's heart, mind, and soul as you confidently send him off.

Okay, I'm hopping down off my soapbox now and grabbing a judgment-free cup of coffee. (That's the kind that has lots of half-and-half and sugar in it because hey, no one's judging.) In the next chapter we'll be talking about social-emotional school readiness. Which is school talk for "whether your kid is ready to make friends and be a friend"—something those school-choice-judging mamas should probably consider.

SEVEN

Social-Emotional Learning 501

Preparing Your Kid for the Grade School Social Scene

SEL 501 Course Syllabus

Professor Erin MacPherson

Welcome to Social Emotional Learning 501, the (almost) graduate-level course where you'll learn how to help your kid be a social rock star. That, and teach your kid to do things like share nice, play well with others, and make a dynamo chocolate chip cookie so you don't have to bake next time your neighbors come over to play.

Course Objectives:

- Help your kids to think, *That must've hurt* instead of, *How's this going to hurt me?* when something bad happens to someone else.

- Teach your kid that being a good friend is a lot more important than being a good student.
- Learn how to empower your kids to stand up to a bully.
- Find out how family traditions can shape your kid's social and emotional skills.

Course Outline:

Section 1: What Exactly Is Social-Emotional Learning?

Section 2: Teaching Empathy

Section 3: Letters or Lessons?

Extra Credit: From the Principal's Office: Protecting Your Kids from Big, Bad Bullies

Bonus Session: It's a Tradition

Final Exam: This time, we're testing your kid and not you. We're giving him a box of fruit snacks and surrounding him with fifteen hungry kindergarteners. Can he figure out how to feed the crowd in a way that no one feels gypped? We shall soon find out.

Section 1: What Exactly Is Social-Emotional Learning?

I have made an important discovery in the world of education, and I'm going to share it with you. (And if this doesn't get me on track for tenure, I don't know what will. Except for actually working at a university, perhaps). Here goes: social-emotional learning is just a buzzword for something moms have been teaching their kids for decades—no, centuries—and it's simple: to have friends, you have to be a friend.

I'm not kidding. You just signed yourself up for a full university course on something that your mom taught you when you were four. Bet you feel you just got duped. But don't shut the book yet! Because even though you've heard this stuff a billion times, it can't hurt to have a little refresher course as you send your kids off to school. After all, the world of modern friendship is, well, a lot like friendship was when you were a kid. Only without cootie catchers and friendship bracelets.

If you ask Mr. Google what social-emotional learning is, he'll list off a bunch of terms like *resilience, responsibility, teachability, courage, discernment, self-control,* and *attitude.* And—are you starting to sense a theme here?—all those terms also happen to be characteristics from The Fifteen Factors. And if that doesn't just wrap things up all nicely and tie them with a big, red bow in your mind, let me tell you this: social-emotional learning has become synonymous with academic success in the educational world. To put that in layman's terms, teachers are finding that kids who show self-control and teachability and other social-emotional assets are more successful in school and life. (Maybe your mom really did know what she was talking about after all!)

Social-emotional learning all boils down to how your kid is able to get along with others—and *others* includes his teachers, his friends, his siblings, his grandparents, and, yes, even you. And if your kids are anything like mine, it's probably pretty obvious that the words "love one another"—the Romans 13 meaning, not the Cher meaning—are lost on them more often than not. Let's just say that that our dinnertime conversation in the last week has revolved around our new mantra: "Love others more than you love your Star Wars light saber."

Think about your own life, and consider where you'd be without your stellar social-emotional skills. Spending five minutes on Facebook practically requires a master's degree in discernment and resiliency. That, and the courage not to tell you-know-who you-know-what about that crazy new rant she's on. And that's before you've even left home! That trip to the playground last week, well, that showed real social-emotional finesse on your part. Not only did you manage to hold your tongue when that competi-mommy told you that her five-year-old aced a middle-school-level reading exam in Arabic, but you shared your picnic blanket with that wide-eyed baby-mom who was clearly making her debut into playground politics. See, you use your social-emotional skills every day, every hour!

But your kid's social-emotional skills probably still need some work. And so, throughout your coursework, you're going to learn how to teach your kid everything your mama ever taught you. Well, not everything—I can't hold a candle to your mom's top-secret spaghetti-sauce recipe. But I can at least help you figure out how to teach your kid how to get along with others in the big, wide world.

Section 2: Teaching Empathy

Just be nice. I say those words at least ninety-six times every day. "Just be nice to your sister." "Could you guys just be nice?" "Just be nice to each other while I make dinner." "Be nice to him; he's just a baby." "Be nice." *"Be nice!"* But—shocker—these words may sound, well, nice, but they actually do very little to teach my kids to actually be nice. In fact, I'm pretty certain that when I say, "Be nice," my kids think, *Oh, she's saying that thing that means we need to look at her wide-eyed and nod our heads, and then we can keep doing exactly what we were doing before.*

Kids don't naturally know how to be nice. And even more, they're often more concerned about getting in trouble than they are about doing the right thing. One hot afternoon this summer, I pulled out our inflatable backyard waterslide while the baby was napping. Joey and Kate dashed outside and proceeded to make up a game where they raced down the slide as quickly as they could to see who could go the fastest. And they were playing so nicely together that I took it as my cue to grab a glass of iced tea and sit on the porch for a few minutes of much-needed downtime. Big mistake.

My quiet reverie was broken when I heard Joey explain to Kate that if he gave her a little friendly push at the top, she'd go faster down the slide. And before I could shout, "Be nice!" he had pushed her off the slide so hard that instead of going down, she went up over the railing and sailed eight feet down into the grass. I watched in horror, frozen, as my four-year-old's wrist bent at an angle that assured me a trip to the ER. And by the time I ran to Kate's side, Joey was nowhere to be found. He had run away to the other side of the house.

Later that night—after Xrays and a cast for her broken arm—I sat down and had a conversation with Joey. Because—just in case you're wondering—that whole push-your-sister-and-run thing really wasn't in line with the type of behavior I like my kids to have. But when I asked him what in the world of tarnation made him think it was a good idea to (a) push his sister on the slide, and (b) hide from me as if I wasn't going to find him, he started to sob. He was clearly distraught. Through his tears, he told me that he was scared he was going to get into trouble and he felt guilty for pushing her too hard and he was afraid she was hurt really bad. All those factors made him want to get away from the whole situation as quickly as he could. So he ran. The poor guy had feelings! And he didn't have the social-emotional skills to do the right thing.

That doesn't make Joey's hit-and-run (or should I say push-and-run) right—trust me: he's heard a lot about it—but it does make it understandable. Because he is still learning about how emotions work—and specifically, he's still learning about empathy. As he ran away, he thought like a little kid (*Yikes! I'm going to get in trouble!*) instead of like a big kid (*Oh no! My sister is hurt! I hope she's okay!*)

I'm convinced that social-emotional learning hinges on empathy. It's not the sole factor—but a kid who shows empathy has the ability to show consideration for how others are feeling. And when you consider others' feelings, characteristics like discernment, self-control, wise decision making, and responsibility are sure to follow. And kids who can do all those things are naturally kids who are good friends.

My kids are (obviously) still learning empathy—but I wanted to share a few tips to help you get started in teaching them to feel deeply for others:

6 Ways to Teach Your Kids to Be Empathetic

1. Respond with empathetic words. When your kid trips and falls, do you (a) smother him with kisses and say he'll be okay, (b) laugh at him and call him clumsy, or (c) tell him to figure out how to walk? If you answered (a), then give yourself a huge pat on the back. Congratulations! You're a mom! Moms have a great sense of empathy—most of us literally feel physical pain when our babies are hurting. But sometimes we're so busy kissing away the pain that we forget to use empathetic words—something that can give our kids the language to express empathy. Try saying, "I feel so sad that you're hurting," or, "I don't like it when you're struggling" to show your kid that your feelings are affected by his pain.

2. Talk about your feelings. I know, I know. The last thing you want to do is tell your kids that you're feeling downright angry that Panera ran out of cinnamon chip cookies before the lunch rush was over. But by sharing your feelings—and putting words to your emotions—your kids learn that (a) mommy has feelings too, and (b) sometimes mommy's feelings are just as irrational as theirs are.

3. Do random acts of kindness. You see that frazzled mom standing behind you in line at Starbucks? The one with must-get-caffeine eyes and four kids hanging on to her legs? Toss an extra ten dollars on your debit card and buy a latte for her and a round of cookies for the troops, and then leave before she finds out who did it. Not only will you make her day—make that, her week—but your kids will see their mama caring about other people's needs, which, by the way, will make *your* week.

4. Give kids a way out. Accidents happen. But by allowing accidents to be learning experiences—chances for your kids to learn how to forgive and move on—you model empathy. So don't get angry next time your kid accidentally trips his sister or knocks over her block tower—instead, calmly ask him how

he thinks he'll be able to make it up to her, and then give him the chance to show empathy.

5. Model patience with little mistakes. I know that blowing bubbles in the milk glass while simultaneously pestering the dog seems like an intentional effort to spill milk all over the floor. But chances are she was probably just having a lot of fun blowing bubbles in the milk glass and didn't think beyond that. Let it slide—toss her a towel; say, "Oops"; and move on.

6. Verbally consider how others feel. The other day I was telling my kids a story about a friend of mine who had lost her dog. And as I explained the situation to my kids, a little bell started *ding, ding*, dinging in my head, reminding me to use the story as a chance to teach empathy. So I changed directions—same story, different word choice—and asked my kids to think about how they would feel if our dog was lost. Suddenly the story really hit home for them. And they were able to really consider how our friend was feeling at that moment.

Section 3: Letters or Lessons?

Mr. Google really threw a curveball at me a few months ago when he started spouting off all these facts about how toddler and pre-schooler reading programs can lead to lower school performance. He even had educational experts from places like Harvard and Tufts and the *TODAY Show* to back him up. I was a bit miffed with him when I heard it too. I mean, how can it hurt your kid to get reading practice at a young age? But once I read the facts, I realized there was something to Mr. Google's claims.

Here's the scoop: It's not that teaching a two-year-old his letters and letter sounds is a problem in and of itself. It's not. But as young kids learn through programs—programs that use TV or a computer as a medium—they lose the opportunity to learn valuable social-emotional skills. To put that in mom terms: as your kid is sitting in front of the TV, learning that b-a-t spells bat, six other kids are outside playing Wiffle ball with a bat and learning all sorts of important skills, like teamwork and respect.

To go deeper, I asked a couple of my kindergarten teacher friends to tell me the scoop on social-emotional skills for kindergarteners. And I learned something really interesting: every teacher I talked to told me that they can tell which kids are going to do well in the first couple weeks of school based on their social-emotional skills. Regardless of how well a kid is reading or counting or spouting off vocabulary in Russian when he enters school, the kids that do well are the ones who know how to share, have emotional conversations, and demonstrate self-control.

My point in all this isn't to chastise you for wasting five dollars on that set of alphabet flash cards—I have boxes of those at home—but simply to remind you to be cognizant of social-emotional skills before you think about academic skills. Yes, you should teach your kids their letters and numbers if they are interested. Yes, you should count the crackers on your kid's plate and the fruit snacks in the box. And yes, you should prepare your kid academically in every way you can. But academic readiness shouldn't be your number-one priority. Because your kid's success is a lot bigger (and better) than a grade on a piece of paper. Or a high score on standardized tests. And that's why I'm going to make up a formula. Based on my educational expertise (and strong knowledge of all things mathematical), I think it makes sense to do two or three social-emotional things to every one academic thing you do with your kids. Here are ten easy ideas to get you started:

10 Simple Ways to Teach Your Kids Social-Emotional Skills

1. Play. Just taking your kids to the park or a playgroup and letting them play with other kids of varying ages teaches valuable social-emotional skills.
2. Read. Expose your children to concepts such as friendship,

respect, kindness, and teamwork through Bible stories and children's books.

3. Give positive reinforcement. Praise your kid for stellar social-emotional behavior.

4. Spend time just talking. Snuggle up on the couch and talk with your kid about whatever it is he wants to talk about. (Bonus: You may just learn something you didn't know about unicorn couture.)

5. Color your feelings. Have your kid draw a "happy" picture, and then have him draw a "sad" picture. Give him time to explain what it is that makes each picture demonstrate those emotions.

6. Play games. Even let your kid lose occasionally.

7. Give him some downtime. Yes, what I'm saying is that when you send your kid upstairs for quiet time so you can get a few minutes' break, you're really doing *him* a favor by helping him understand solitude and quiet time with God.

8. Listen to Christian music. Memorize the lyrics, and sing together. Often.

9. Give your kid a redo. When he makes a little mistake—a snappy comment or ignored command—tell him to try again to do it right.

10. Do a project together. If you're a DIYer, this could mean building a playhouse or a swing set from the ground up. Or, if you'd prefer not to spend your entire weekend trucking back and forth between your house and Lowes—try tackling a simpler project, like organizing the junk drawer or planting a flower bed.

· ·

From the Principal's Office

Extra Credit: Protecting Your Kids from Big, Bad Bullies
by Ellen Schuknecht

Bullying is a big, massive, social-emotional issue for school-aged kids. It occurs more often than you think—I see it on almost a weekly basis at the private Christian school where I work. But what worries me most is the bullying I *don't* see. Blatant, obvious bullies are often caught and stopped. But behind the scenes at every school, there are kids who are being victimized by sly and skilled bullies who know exactly what to do to keep their actions under the table. These kids often suffer for months, or even years, before they get the help they need.

Since bullying behavior can go unnoticed by even vigilant adults, I've realized that the best defense for bullying is actually offense. I teach my students—and my grandchildren—how to handle bullying behavior on their own so that if a bully targets them, they react in a way that stops the bullying before it can get bad. Here are the three tricks I teach kids:

- Trick one: Put on your no-feelings face. Bullies are looking for an emotional reaction—so I teach kids to take away their power by stripping all emotion from their expression. The second a bully engages in bullying behavior, I tell them to put on their no-feelings face—not sad, not mad, not happy, not angry. Just blank. It takes a bit of practice to figure out a no-feelings face, so I have my kids practice in the mirror so they know exactly what to do when bullying behavior strikes.
- Trick two: Keep a few easy phrases in your back pocket. Fighting fire with fire usually means that someone gets burned. And fighting fire with sugar simply melts the sugar. So I teach kids to fight fire with water—and throw soothing words at a bully and then just walk away. Teach your kids a few simple, soothing, and totally nonemotional expressions, like "That's interesting" or "Thanks for telling me that" that they can keep in their back pockets to toss at a bully when mean words are spoken.
- Trick three: Tell a safe adult in writing. Kids are terrified of being labeled a tattletale, or of an adult not believing them. So I teach my kids to write a note (or draw a picture if they are young) about what happened and then to give the note to one safe adult. This not only allows kids to process what happened, but also assures that a victim doesn't go unnoticed.

I've found that by empowering victims to handle bullies in a safe and proactive manner, the bullying incidents at our school have declined. Additionally, we've been able to put a stop to many situations before they got out of hand and someone got hurt. And because of this, I think all parents—especially parents of young kids— should teach their kids how to handle a bullying situation before they go to school. All it takes is three simple tricks. (Which, by the way, is about seven less steps than it takes to tie a shoe.)

· ·

Bonus Session: It's a Tradition

The idea for Cookie Fridays started because I don't like to go grocery shopping. (Well, that and because I'll take any excuse to eat cookies.) It was a Friday afternoon, and I realized I was completely out of anything that resembled an after-school snack. No fruit or veggies in the fridge. No prewrapped packages or fruit snacks or chocolate chip granola bars in the pantry. And so, instead of serving my kids scrambled eggs and nondairy creamer for their snack, I took them down to Whole Foods and let them each pick a cookie.

And since the thought of loading three kids back into the car a mere ten minutes after I unloaded them made me want to fall asleep right there on the spot, I nabbed a couple of cartons of milk and a high chair and we set up shop at a table in the middle of the café. And as we sat there savoring those cookies bite by bite, I realized that this was different from the normal crumb-fueled fury of snack time at home. We talked about our week's highs and lows and our plans for the weekend. We discussed our favorite types of cookies. We even took a few minutes to muse about the weather. And even though Will kept trying to swipe the juice box off the table next to us, I was feeling pretty cool, calm, and collected. Well, as cool, calm, and collected as a mom can be in a public place with three kids.

So we made it a tradition: every Friday after school we head to a bakery and we each pick a cookie. And then we sit with cartons of milk and just talk. And enjoy a few minutes of time together before the weekend begins. And there's a reason I'm telling you this (beyond letting you know that I'm a sucker for anything chocolate chip)—I'm positive that Cookie Fridays have helped grow my kids' social-emotional skills. Not only do these outings serve as something to look forward to each week, but as time has passed, my kids have learned how to share their feelings with me and each other, to talk about events in their lives, and even how to savor slow conversation and time together.

Think back to your own childhood. Some of my most treasured memories involve the traditions we had as a family. I remember sitting around the fire during Advent while my mom played Christmas tunes on the piano and just feeling so loved, so cherished, and a part of something that was so much bigger than me. That's what a tradition does—it gives your kid an anchor to hold on to when life gets tough, a place where he can go to feel safe, cherished, and loved.

And so, before we finish this course, I have a final assignment for you. It's actually a pretty easy one (I know that essay on teaching empathy probably did you in). I want you to think of one small family tradition that you can start that will help your kids grow social-emotional skills. It doesn't have to be anything big or elaborate—but just one small thing you can do on a regular basis that will help your kids' social-emotional learning in a place that's safe. A place where they'll feel cherished and loved. And if that place involves cookies, well, even better.

10 Family Traditions That Build Social-Emotional Skills

1. Serve together. My friend Janel's family dedicates one Saturday every month to doing a service project together. At

Christmastime they put together Operation Christmas Child boxes. In the spring they help with a widow's spring cleaning. In the summer they help clean up a park.

2. Un-dinner. When I was a kid, my mom didn't cook on Sunday nights. Instead, each of us was in charge of making our own "un-dinner"—and the best part was that we could make whatever we wanted. So we'd all gather in the kitchen around five thirty to start creating our un-dinner creations—often trying to out-un-dinner each other. There was a period of time (that lasted six or seven years) when my brother and I ate ice cream sundaes every week—and another period of time when gummy bears and popcorn were the course du jour. But regardless of what we ate, we always had fun sitting at the (unset) table and talking about how our crazy (read: brilliant) mom was letting us have ice cream for dinner.

3. Highs and lows. My friend Sarah has each member of her family share his or her high point and low point of the day over family dinner each night. She says that even her two-year-old has gotten in on it—even though her daily high often involves Dora or the potty.

4. Friday Night Lights Off. Order pizza and rent a family movie, and spend Friday nights snuggling together on the couch.

5. Get puzzled. Set up a puzzle in an out-of-the-way place, and work on it together whenever you get the chance. One rule: no one can ever work alone.

6. Keep a family bucket list. Have your kids and your husband help you write a list of all of the fun family activities you'd like to do. Then make it your goal to cross one thing off your bucket list every month.

7. Get some exercise. Make it your family tradition to go on a walk through your neighborhood every evening after dinner—rain or shine.

8. Saturday morning breakfast. There's nothing like a lazy

Saturday morning—except maybe a lazy Saturday morning that involves pancakes. If you don't feel like making pancakes, try Saturday morning doughnuts or Saturday mornings at the diner. What you eat isn't important—but eating together is.

9. Have a sleepover. Set aside a night every so often for a family sleepover in your backyard or on your living room floor.

10. Read the Bible together. When I was a kid, my grandfather kept his Bible in the top drawer of the dining room hutch. Every morning before breakfast, he pulled it out and read a passage to the family, then while they ate, the kids talked about what the verse meant to them. Talk about finding a genius way to avoid the "my eggs are yummier than your eggs" drama and to give your kids something real to think about at the same time.

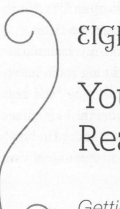

EIGHT

Your Kindergarten-Readiness Checklist

*Getting Your Kid Academically
Ready for School*

What's not to love about a good, old-fashioned checklist? I love the thrill of chasing down yet another to-do and conquering it with the force of my sheer willpower and the dash of a red pen. And, so, as you can imagine, when a guest speaker at my MOPS group passed out a kindergarten-readiness checklist, I was on it like a sleep-deprived mama on coffee. I wasn't going to let a day pass without considering how I could prepare my kids for the future. Who cared that my oldest was only two? We were going to start getting ready for kindergarten.

After laminating the list and posting it on the fridge, I started to consider—okay, obsess—about the massive amount of knowledge my kids would need to possess before they started school. I mean, not only did they need to know their letters and numbers, but they also should know how to do crazy ridiculous things, like pee in the potty, button their own jackets, and—get this—put the straw in their own juice boxes. How were we ever going to get there?

I'm sure you can guess what happened next. I worked diligently for three years to make sure my kid mastered every skill on the list so he could enter kindergarten 100 percent prepared and ready. Or maybe it didn't go exactly like that. The truth is that I obsessed for a few weeks before the thrill wore off. Then I set the list aside, it got lost in a pile of other, equally important papers on my desk, and I completely forgot about said list until the night before Joey entered kindergarten. I dug it out of the drawer, and after reading it, I had a moment of panic as I tried to rationalize to myself that my baby was really, truly ready to head off to school:

- Listens to adults talking without interrupting. *(Maybe if the adult is talking about Legos or intergalactic droid battles.)*
- Recognizes rhyming words. *(Does singing "Jesus Loves Me" count?)*
- Has a basic understanding of how to use scissors. *(Wait! They're going to let my kid use scissors?! He's only five!)*
- Has a general understanding of the times of the day. *(He doesn't get that 5:45 a.m. is not a time to be awake, so nope.)*
- Manages bathroom needs. *(Score! One point for mommy and her stellar potty training skills.)*
- Is able to button pants and fasten belt after using bathroom. *(They don't have to be buttoned perfectly, right?)*
- Can identify some letters, shapes, and numbers. *(Check, check, and check. Keyword here: some.)*
- Understands that actions have both cause and effect. *(Yeah, right.)*
- Is able to separate from parents without tears. *(Most of the time.)*
- Can bounce a ball. *(I'm an adult, and I can't even do that.)*

When I realized it was too late to drag Joey out of bed for an all-night kindergarten-readiness cramming session, I did the rational thing and moped around the living room, crying about how my son was going to be behind on the first day of school. And my sweet husband (who happens to have a fancy education degree that proves he knows something about schooling) reminded me that while it'd be nice if our kids were perfectly prepared for kindergarten on the first day, the truth is, that it's an impossible task.

No kid in the history of the world has started school knowing everything he needed to know to start school. And even if a kid did happen to grow up in a house with a mama who had the tenacity to stick to the kindergarten-readiness checklist until every item was checked off, he would still probably forget everything he knew the second he walked into the door of the school. It's Murphy's (or should I say, MacPherson's) law of kindergarten readiness.

My point? (Yes, I have a point!) You should do whatever you can to help your kid get ready for school. You should teach him about letters and numbers and shapes and how to button and zip his pants so he doesn't walk around with his fly open all day. But this isn't something to obsess about. Because that checklist isn't as important as what's going on in your kid's heart. But I've already said that a billion times, haven't I? And I hope it's starting to sink in.

Because if the only thing you do to get your kid ready for school is work on The Fifteen Factors, then you're doing well. No, better than well. You're doing *great*. And I can assure you that if your kid enters school knowing who he is before God and what really matters in life, he will be successful.

But practically speaking, there are things you can do to help your kid get prepared for school—both academically and socially. And for the next couple of chapters, I'm going to help you work through those things. It's a kindergarten-readiness checklist of sorts—a random assortments of my thoughts, tips, and learnings that I hope will help you as you as you help your kid get ready for school. First up, it's academic readiness. And in the next chapter we'll continue this talk as I show you how to communicate with your kid. Ready to get started checking things off your checklist?

· ·

Time-Out for Mom

For When You're Praying for Your Kid's Mind

"I pray that you, being rooted and established in love, may have power, together with all the Lord's holy people, to grasp how wide and long and high and deep is the love of Christ." (Ephesians 3:17–18)

Lord Jesus, my kid's mind is soaking in so much knowledge right now. Reading and math and science fill his mind—and that's a wonderful thing. But I want him to know You. Lord, as he learns and grows, fill him with Your love. Reveal Yourself to him so he can fully grasp the power of Your saving love, Your freely given grace, and Your perfect hope—so that as he grows in knowledge, he grows most of all in his understanding of You as his God and Savior. Amen

· ·

Considering Your Kid's Learning Personality

I know Joey and Kate share the same genes. (Mostly because I carried them in my womb for nine months each—that's a pretty good indicator.) They have the same nose, the same wide-eyed smile, and a shared love of all things chocolate. But when it comes to academics, they couldn't be more different.

Kate is a reader. She loves letters and words and books and stories. And by the time she was two, she could point out the letters in her name when we read *Chicka Chicka Boom Boom*. She's naturally drawn to all things literary—a girl after her mama's heart—so teaching her to read and write has been easy. But Joey?

Not so much. I remember one day when he was about four, I got out the letter magnets and we started arranging them on the fridge to make words. I'd spell "DOG" and Joey would spell "SDREGDCS" and then proudly exclaim that he had done it! And perfectly!

Finally, after much frustration, I realized our problem: Joey is mathematical in nature. And where I saw letters and words, he saw patterns. So spelling SDREGDCS with a red, green, blue, yellow pattern looked perfect to him. And it looked like gibberish to me. I tried again and again to teach Joey to recognize letters and words, and he simply wasn't interested. Or willing to even try.

On the flip side, Joey is naturally inclined toward anything pattern-oriented—math, science, engineering, organizing. The kid can build with Legos with the best of them. And if you ask him to count out money or figure out a mathematical solution to organizing the pantry, he's all over it. Okay, so maybe not with the pantry thing, but wouldn't that be great?

One day I dumped a bag of dry beans into a bowl and asked Joey and Kate to put them in groups of ten. Joey loved it. He spent hours counting and sorting beans. Kate? She counted out one pile and then looked up at me as if I were crazy. And then, with a look of desperation, she said, "Mom, I don't understand why beans have anything to do with learning." Counting beans just isn't her cup of tea. Technically, it's not mine either, so I don't blame the girl.

Your kid has a natural, God-given learning personality—and while that doesn't mean he'll necessarily struggle in other areas, it does mean that his greatest successes and greatest enjoyment will come from the things he's naturally good at. I've seen that very clearly with Joey since he started school. I've been fortunate in that he's picked up reading fairly quickly since he started school—he now loves books and loves to read—but his favorite subject is still math. And his math homework is always the work that he chooses to do first.

Just as I told you earlier, in chapter 3, that you should encourage The Fifteen Factor characteristics toward which your kid is naturally inclined, you should also work to encourage your kid in his natural areas of interest. And while that doesn't mean ignoring other areas, it does mean allowing your kid to learn his way instead of your way. Even if that means counting beans.

. . . .

From the Principal's Office

Using Your Kid's God-Given Talents to Prepare Him for School
by Ellen Schuknecht

I am always intrigued by how God creates each kid—even kids from the same family and background—with his or her own unique gifts, talents, and strengths. Different kids are motivated in different ways—often based on their individual interests and God-given talents—and therefore, different kids are going to learn in different ways. By allowing his interests to drive your efforts as you work to get your kid ready to start school, you can not only help him learn what he wants to learn about, but also give him the basis to start learning skills he isn't naturally inclined to learn. Here are some tips to help you do that:

∽ A competitive kid will enjoy activities that are measurable and provide immediate feedback. To increase interest in more subjective areas, like reading or writing, give him a challenge like, "See how many letters you can write in five minutes," or "Yesterday, you were able to find six letters you recognized in this story. Let's see if you can find seven today."

∽ An artistic, creative kid who would write and draw all day long but resist doing the sheet of "boring" math problems would benefit from learning about how creatively God put together the universe. Show him a scale of the solar system and discuss how creatively mathematical our world is.

- An athletic kid who doesn't like to sit still for more than three seconds will do better when you mix things up. Create learning centers where he can spend five minutes practicing his letters and then run to the next room to spend five minutes counting rocks and then run outside and spend five minutes finding objects that start with the letter S.
- For your math-minded kid who would rather play Legos or blocks, set up a comfy reading corner in your house with a bean bag chair, a lamp, a bookshelf, and a checklist of books he can check off when he finishes reading them.
- Let your musical kid count the drumbeats in his favorite songs and record them on a sheet of paper.
- A "black-and-white," detail-oriented child may be reluctant to embark on artistic endeavors—so give him colored pencils and ask him to draw ten stars with different colors. Then ask him to try to make different color combinations with dots or circles on his paper.

Teaching Your Kid Reading

Reading is a big deal during the first few years of school. In fact, I'll go as far as to say it's the one and only thing your kids really need to learn in kindergarten. Because the ability to read transfers to just about every subject he will ever learn in school. Plus, the avid reader in me has to point out that a lifetime love of reading leads to, well, the chance to devour a lot of great books and learn a lot about just about everything in the process.

But let me also reassure you that if your kid enters kindergarten without a strong grasp of reading, he or she will probably be just fine. As I said earlier, Joey isn't a "letters and words" person. So, while I tried—hard—to teach him to read before kindergarten, I failed miserably. He entered kindergarten with a very rudimentary understanding of reading. And I was worried that would transfer to academic struggles for the rest of his school year.

But it didn't. Joey picked up reading in school pretty quickly, regardless of his preparedness. His strong understanding (and love) of math really helped him as he realized that letters form patterns to make words. Plus, his love of being read to and of hearing stories carried him as he learned to read. So while you may worry if your kid doesn't know the letters or letter sounds or how to read complex dissertations before he enters school, let me reassure you: it's important—but not *that* important.

So how can you get your kid ready to read without causing a lot of undue stress? One of the best ways is to read to your kid, and often. There is no better way to encourage a love of books—a love of books that will often manifest itself in a love of reading. But there are also other low-stress things you can do to help jump-start his reading skills. Here are ten easy ways:

10 Easy Ways to Give Your Kid a Jump Start on Reading

1. Read novels. Children's books are great—we read them all the time—but there's something to be said for getting wrapped up in a good novel. And starting at about age four or five, kids are ready to follow complex, read-aloud stories over time. Last year we read *The Lion, the Witch and the Wardrobe* by C. S. Lewis to our kids, and while we did have to stop to check their understanding from time to time, they absolutely loved it.

2. Stop and ask questions. When reading stories to your kids, ask them about the characters or how they feel about a certain situation, giving them the chance to think critically about what's happening instead of just hearing about it. This is the precursor to reading comprehension—a skill they'll learn a lot about in the years to come.

3. Use your computer. Let Mr. Google babysit for a while—I mean, let Mr. Google give you a hand with kindergarten readiness—and introduce your kid to literacy-learning websites like Starfall.com and BrainPOP.com. While these are no substitutes for you actually reading to your kids, they're nice supplements that also give you a break.

4. Make alphabet soup. Anytime you can expose your kids to letters, you're giving them basic reading skills. So make alphabet soup for lunch, or spell their names with blueberries on their breakfast plates.

5. Play games with letters. We play a game in the car where we see who can spell the letters in his or her name the fastest by finding them on roadside signs. So I try to find the letters E-R-I-N while Joey tries to find J-O-E-Y. Once your kid gets really good at his own name, see if he can find other words—*dog, cat, fish*—or if he's really good, the whole alphabet.

6. Let your kid read on his own. Bedtime means lights-out at our house—no more water, no more trips to the potty, and certainly no getting out of bed because they want to check if the fairy monster in the closet is still there. But we do have one exception: if our kids aren't tired, we allow them to turn on a flashlight and look at books. They love looking through books at their own pace, and now that they're learning to read, they love it even more. (Bonus: if they're busy reading, they won't be tempted to come downstairs to see what you and daddy are up to.)

7. Point out letters. Start out with the first letter in your kid's name and point it out every time you see it—in books, on signs, at the mall. Then start pointing out other letters and help build letter recognition.

8. Go to the library or the bookstore. To my kids, the ultimate Saturday afternoon adventure is a trip to the bookstore. And this may be partially because I always get them vanilla milk

in the coffee shop, but it's also because they love looking at all the books on the shelves.

9. Get books your kid is going to like. This may sound obvious—but your kid will probably like books about things he's interested in. Which means *Tea Time with Fluffy the Rainbow Teddy* may not resonate with certain kids as well as, say, *Strike at the Booger Factory* and *Captain Dirty Socks and His Adventures at the Mud Pit.*

10. Read poetry. Joey's teacher (who happens to be a reading specialist) told me that fluency—the ability to read with a rhythm—tends to be significantly higher in kids who have been exposed to poetry. So find books with a cadence—Shel Silverstein is a favorite at our house—and start reading to the beat.

Teaching Your Kid About Math

You probably thought you were done thinking about things like fractions and decimals and elliptical runners when you passed algebra class, didn't you? But surprise! Now your kid is going to school—which means you get to learn all those things again. Now, I have to acquiesce to the fact that there may be some engineers, math teachers, and general math nerds reading this who actually *like* math—in which case this whole teaching-your-kid-math thing sounds fun to you—but for literary-minded girls like me, it's absolutely terrifying.

Terrifying, but doable. It turns out that kindergarten math isn't all that hard. In fact, I was able to stumble through the entire year of helping Joey with his math homework without once enlisting the help of my math-teacher dad. Go me! And as you start the kindergarten readiness process, I want to assure you that there's not a single quadratic equation on the kindergarten curriculum. In my state, at least. So, for now, you can sit back, relax, and try some of these easy, practical ways to help your kid start learning math.

10 Easy Ways to Give Your Kids
a Jump Start in Math

1. Play games. Board games and card games require complex mathematical thinking skills—which means your kid is thinking, *Playtime with mom,* and you're thinking, *Look at me homeschooling!*

2. Count beans (and other things.) Gather up small objects—beans, pasta, crayons—and have your kid count them and then sort them into piles. Sounds simple, but your kid will gain valuable counting and sorting skills—not to mention cleaning skills when he helps you sweep up the beans that "accidentally" spilled all over the floor.

3. Don't do math for your kid. Next time your kid asks for a sixteen-dollar game at Target, don't just say no. Instead, ask him to figure out how much money he has and how much extra money he'll need to earn in order to buy it. (By the by, the same strategy works with husbands wanting to buy sixteen-hundred-dollar LCD television sets.)

4. Recruit some help in the kitchen. It's bizarre how much I like cooking, considering how much math it involves. And by the time I get done measuring and counting and dividing fractions to figure out how much of the pie I can swipe before my husband gets home, it's a wonder I ever get any food on a plate at all. But I digress. Recruit your kid to help measure ingredients or put four strawberries on each plate and he'll gain valuable math skills. And you'll gain a kitchen helper who understands that three eggplants plus two heads of lettuce really doesn't add up to dinner.

5. Play games in the car. See if your kid can find ten street signs. Or four orange cones. Or six drive-thru coffee shops. (Actually, when it comes to drive-thru coffee shops, one will probably suffice.)

6. Let them sort. In a moment of rainy-day desperation a few

weeks ago, I handed Joey a jar or change and asked him to sort it into piles of pennies, nickels, quarters, and dimes and then let me know how many of each coin I had. And what would've been my worst form of childhood torture became his favorite activity *ever*. He asked me if he could do it again the next day just to see if the numbers had changed.

7. Set the timer. Telling time is—*shh!*—math. So, even when you don't have to set the timer (you know: to scare him into eating his vegetables), set it to help him get a sense of time. Tell him you'll read to him for ten more minutes and then you guys can go color. Or let him know that school starts in twenty minutes, so you'll be leaving in five.

8. Give your kid an allowance. We give our kids a dollar every week for every year of age. So Joey gets six bucks. Kate gets five. But then things get complicated. Every week they have to use their budding math skills to sort their money into a "give to Jesus" pile, a "save for later" pile, and a "save for me" pile. Oh, and if they do something like forget to feed the dog, they also have a "pay mom to do my chores for me" pile.

9. Build with blocks. See if your kid can make a tower that's ten blocks high. Then see if he can make one that's eight blocks high. I bet after some thought, he may even be able to tell you which one is taller. An engineer in the making, that kid.

10. Keep up your calendar. I know, I know; if you really need to know the date, you can just check your iPhone. But your kid can't. So keep a paper calendar on the wall, and mark off important events and dates to help give your kid a sense of the passage of time.

Other Things Your Kid May Need to Know

Let's pretend for a second that you gave birth to a mega-genius who knew his letters before he was sleeping through the night. Or who knew how to count backward by sixes from 1,224 before he turned four. Well then, you're going to need some other things to teach your kid before he heads off to school. And while the previous chapter on social and emotional learning is a good place to start, I figured you overachiever parents out there—you know who you are—may need something else to do during your free time. Here are a few other things that it wouldn't hurt for your kid to know:

- How to pack his own lunch. (And while he's at it, perhaps how to whip up a nice grilled chicken salad for your lunch as well.)
- How to rub hot chocolate stains out of his favorite T-shirt so he can wear it two (or six) days in a row.
- How to determine if an offering in the hot lunch line is a fruit, a vegetable, or a dessert.
- How to get dressed for school in 4.3 seconds flat (for those days that you miss your alarm).
- How to get dressed for school as slowly as possible (for those days that he wakes up at 4:34 in the morning and you have to find something for him to do so you can grab a few more z's).
- How to fit four water bottles and two lunch boxes into one backpack for those days when he finally remembers to bring all his stuff home.
- How to clean six-day-old food out of lunch boxes.
- How to write his name—first and last in Sharpie—on everything he owns. Including his pencil erasers.
- How to say, "My mom taught me that" every time he does something amazing.

NINƐ

Great Communicators Anonymous

Encouraging The Fifteen Factors with Your Words

'm starting a club. I think I'll call it Great Communicators Anonymous (GCA). And it will be for all of us moms who—through no fault of our own—have to deal with selective listeners and conversation-avoiders on a daily basis. It'll be great fun. We can sit around and discuss all the ways that our obvious communicative genius is being wasted on kids (and husbands) who only seem to hear about a quarter of what we say. And even when they do hear it, they only seem to comprehend 10 percent of what they take in. I just shared my brilliant idea with my husband and he isn't quite as excited about it as I am. In fact, he suggested that perhaps a better name for my little group would be "Naggers Anonymous." See what I'm up against? He doesn't even seem to care that his little comment landed him on GCA's blacklist for life. Whatever. His loss.

Anyway, the inspiration for my little idea came last week when I asked my kids to do a simple chore. They were playing UNO together when I asked them to put the game away and go clean their rooms. I spoke very slowly, plainly, and clearly—there wasn't a dangling participle or mixed metaphor in sight—but they still must have misunderstood what I said because they both just sat there and continued to play their game. As if they hadn't heard my request at all.

I waited a few seconds and tried again. "Let's go clean our rooms, and once we're done, maybe we can all play UNO together." Still nothing. Not even a sideways glance. Of course, I eventually did get them to get up and clean their rooms. (Turns out that threatening to load all their toys into garbage bags and give them to Goodwill works wonders in motivating kids to clean their rooms.) But it took me asking them several times.

This lack of communication skills (theirs, not mine, of course) manifests itself in other ways as well. It's not just when I'm asking them to do something. It's also when I'm just talking to them. I asked my son Joey how his day at school was the other day and he looked at me as if I had just asked him to eat boiled tofu and mushy peas for dinner. He grunted, "Fine, Mo-om," and then he told me with an exasperated sigh that he was pretty tired from the day. And maybe I could talk to Daddy later if I really felt like talking so much.

In our house there is (at times) a communication gap between me and my kids. To be entirely fair, I can tell you that certain kids (read: Joey) have a harder time communicating than others (read: Kate), but both of my big kids seem to suffer bouts of selective listening, sentence misunderstanding, and plain, old-fashioned I'm-going-to-ignore-mom-itis. But I want this to change. I want to communicate with my kids in a meaningful way! And I admit that there are (many) times when I don't know how to do that. But I've been working on it. And in this chapter, I'm going to share what I've learned about how good communication—okay, *great* communication (we are, after all,

GCA) can not only lead to good relationships with our kids, but also help them to grow in many of The Fifteen Factors—vision, resiliency, wise decision making, responsibility, focus, godly knowledge, discernment, honesty, and a positive attitude, to name a few.

Amp Up the Communication

I think one of the initiation rituals for all new members of GCA will be to ask them to communicate more with their kids. I know that seems a bit oxymoronical (yes, that's a word . . . I made it up myself) since older kids need less direct because-I-said-so guidance. But hear me out. I didn't say you needed to talk *at* your kid more. I didn't even say you needed to tell your kid more about life or God or school. I said you needed to *communicate* more. Or at least more in depth. Because it's through real, meaningful conversation—and through time to contemplate and disseminate information—that kids can begin to truly understand who they are and who God intends them to be.

A few months ago I got a call from Joey's teacher about an incident involving an eraser and some sort of projectile launcher that landed an eraser into another kid's forehead. Typical boy stuff. But when the teacher confronted the boys involved, Joey lied to his face and told him he knew nothing about it. He flat-out lied to his teacher. *Fantastic.* (That's heavy sarcasm there, just in case you can't read between the lines.)

When Joey got home from school, I wanted to thump *him* on the head and tell him exactly what I thought about his eraser-flinging, kid-hurting lies. I mean, really, he knew better! I have taught him from day one that lying *and* eraser flinging are wrong. But instead I oh-so-calmly asked him what happened. And he oh-so-calmly responded by telling me that he didn't want to get into trouble so he told his teacher he didn't do it. And that was that.

Of course, that *wasn't* that, as far as I was concerned. But as I talked with Joey more, I realized that while I had drilled him over and over again with the fact that lying was wrong, he had clearly never internalized the concept. Because in his five-year-old mind, lying was kind of a gray area. He knew it wasn't good. But it was also a necessary evil to getting what he wanted. (Which, in this case, was avoiding trouble with this teacher.)

After realizing that this was more than a simple white lie, but instead a matter of the heart, we had a long conversation about what had happened. We talked about how God is truth and how that even when the truth may lead to a consequence, it's always better than an untruth. And I think he (eventually) got it.

And I learned something too: I have to do more than just tell my kids what's right and wrong. I have to give them tools to be able to internalize the The Fifteen Factors so they can navigate the black, white, and gray areas in the world on their own. Just talking isn't enough. But by asking the tough questions and giving them the (guided) space to work out their own thoughts and feelings, I'm giving my kids the tools they need to think and act independently.

· ·

Time-Out for Mom

For When You're Learning to Communicate with Your Kids

"A good man brings good things out of the good stored up in his heart, and an evil man brings evil things out of the evil stored up in his heart. For the mouth speaks what the heart is full of." (Luke 6:45)

Lord Jesus, I want to talk to my kids in a way that brings them closer to You. Please fill me with the words that will help them learn and grow and thrive. Erase any words from my mouth that are destructive or hurtful. You say that out of the abundance of our hearts, our mouths speak. Fill my heart with You, so that my words will be full of an abundance of Your grace, Your hope, and Your love. Amen.

. . . .

Nag Less, Inspire More

I don't want to be the one to have to break it to you, but nagging your kids just doesn't work. I know it *seems* as if it would work—I mean, what could possibly be more inspiring than someone telling you what to do, over and over?—but for some reason, kids tend to just ignore nagging mothers. Which means the things you're wanting to get done aren't getting done.

Big kids have busy lives. My first grader has a spelling test every week and twenty minutes of individual reading practice every night. In addition to that, he has math practice, book reports, and soccer games. Plus—mean mom that I am—I tend to prefer it when he keeps his room at least somewhat clean. And I'll admit: it's a lot for a six-year-old to do. And in moments of desperation (read: every afternoon), I tend to resort to nagging. But as I said, that's simply not working. He ignores me and still doesn't get his homework or chores done. How can we as parents teach our kids responsibility—and make sure they get things done—without getting on their case every five minutes? I asked my mom for ideas. Here's what she said:

4 Ways to Inspire Your Kids to Get Things Done Without Nagging Them

1. Make a schedule.

My husband is a fly-by-the-seat-of-his-work-pants kind of guy. I'm more of an iron-my-work-pants-a-week-in-advance kind of girl. And so, from the day we got married, we've been in a sort of scheduled-versus-unscheduled tug-of-war. Now that we have kids,

I'm finally winning. Back before we had kids, I couldn't really argue with him when he told me to hop in the car after work on a Friday and drove us to San Francisco (we lived in Portland) for the weekend. Because it was fun. But now? A spontaneous trip to the grocery store has long-term ramifications. So I've scheduled our kids' lives. The hour before dinner is homework time (and for kids who don't have homework, it's coloring time). The thirty minutes before bed is reading time. And Saturday mornings are for picking up every single toy that has made its way downstairs and into my living room during the week. It works for us. My kids may whine occasionally, but they know that we keep to this schedule, and there's no use trying to change it. I knew I was right all along, but I have to admit it's pretty nice to finally have proof.

2. Take mini-breaks.

All work and no play make for cranky kids and cranky moms—obviously—but a messy house and unfolded laundry and undone homework also make for cranky kids and moms. In order to keep my own sanity, I always give myself little mini-breaks throughout the day. A hot mug of coffee once I finish the laundry or a Dove chocolate because I managed to stop a sibling fight without blowing my top. Okay, so all my breaks involve food, but regardless, a few minutes' break works wonders for my spirit—and my energy. And I've noticed it does the same thing for my kids. When my kids are doing homework, I track time for about ten minutes and then have them hop up for a mini-break. I'll turn on a dance song and we'll rock out for a minute, or I'll have them run as fast as they can to the slide, go down it once, and then come back. That thirty-second change of pace makes a huge difference in their motivation to work.

3. Don't be afraid to cut back.

I can't believe I'm actually going to say this out loud and in public but—deep breath—it's okay if your kid's life isn't perfect. He doesn't have to live in a perfectly clean room or do every assignment perfectly or turn in extra credit work every other day. And while all these things are important and should take priority—they aren't more important than your kid's emotional health. If you sense your kid shutting down because homework or housework or schoolwork is getting too stressful, stop. Go to bed or go on a walk or grab dinner. A missed assignment or unmade bed is hardly a major issue in the whole scheme of things—but a stressed and worn-out kid is.

4. Help your kid come up with working solutions.

My son Joey has about twelve billion Lego mini-figures (give or take a billion). Up until two weeks ago, these mini-figures lived in a plastic bin in Joey's room. Wait; that's a lie. The mini-figures lived on the floor, because Joey never, ever, ever put them into the plastic bin. So after a very painful incident that involved a sword-wielding mini-figure and my foot, I snapped. And when I oh-so-sweetly explained to him that if he didn't start picking them up in the next nanosecond, I was going to give the entire collection to his younger cousin, he looked at me with big brown eyes and explained that he simply couldn't put them away. He went on to explain that the Star Wars mini-figures and the Ninja mini-figures didn't like living in the plastic bin with the police and astronaut mini-figures. Of course. Three small bins later, Joey's floor was spotless. And it's stayed spotless—because, as Joey told me, "Mini-figures are much happier when they aren't forced to live with creatures from other planets." The takeaway here—aside from the all-important realization that Jabba the Hutt doesn't mix with Lego Police—is that by giving kids the freedom to help solve problems and organize their own lives, you may just inspire them to do it on their own.

Be Your Kid's Go-to Gal

This next section isn't for the faint of heart. In fact, you may want to sit down as you read this, because it isn't pretty. Here goes.

Last year, my friend Marcy's six-year-old daughter, Liza, came home from school one day and nonchalantly asked, "Mommy, what's sex?" After Marcy wiped up the coffee she had spit out when she heard her daughter's question, she managed to choke out the words to ask her where she had heard about *that*. Liza explained that she had overheard some "big kids" (read: fifth graders) on the playground, talking about how they couldn't wait to have sex and how fun it was going to be. And Liza—always one for a good time—thought it might be something she wanted to do too.

Your kid is going to hear things. And these things aren't exactly the types of things you discuss at family dinner. There's no way to shelter your kid from being exposed to these things—even if he doesn't go to school, he'll hear things at the gym, on the subway, or at the mall. Or he'll just use his newfound reading skills to read about them on magazine covers while you're standing in line at Target.

You just can't protect your kid from the world. You can, however, help your kid be ready to face these situations in a way that pleases God. Think of it this way: if your kid were Liza, would you rather she asked you, or the fifth graders on the playground, for clarification. Obviously, the answer is you. You want to be the one they turn to for explanations! Then you can help shape their minds and show them how God truly intended them to live.

This whole scenario—totally freak-out-worthy as it is—is actually a good thing. In fact—as crazy as it seems—I hope something similar happens to one of my kids someday. (Well, not exactly similar—poor Marcy!) But it's situations like this where you have the opportunity to dig deep with your kids and show them that they can trust you with their questions. And they can believe you to give them honest answers. Because you want them to come to you first, each and every time they hear something that's confusing, strange, or downright disturbing. Here are some tips on how to become your kid's go-to-gal:

4 Ways to Make Sure Your Kid Comes to You First with Tough Questions

1. Never freak out in front of your kid.

I get that the mere thought of your kid hearing about you-know-what or you-know-who makes you hyperventilate. But go into the bathroom and close the door before you do, because the last thing you want your kid to start thinking is that he shouldn't share things with you because you might freak out. So take a deep breath and smile—and don't let your kid know that you're cringing inside.

2. Be honest and forthcoming (albeit age-appropriately).

I tell my kids the truth—about just about everything. Okay, so I don't just jump out there and tell them about war or sex or drugs out of the blue, but if they ask, I do my best to give them an honest answer. So when my son asked me how his baby brother got into my tummy, I tiptoed around the issue for a while and then called my mom. And then I called my best friend to make sure what my mom said sounded right. But eventually, I came up with an honest answer for my son: God takes a seed from a daddy and a seed from a mommy and puts them together to create a new baby that grows inside the mommy's uterus. And—thankfully—he accepted my answer without asking *how* the seeds got into the mommy. For now, at least. But when that question comes, I'll have to find a way to be honest again. Because I want my son to trust that when he asks me questions, I'm going to answer him.

3. Don't be afraid to wait.

You do not have to answer all questions the second they are asked. As I said earlier, I stumbled around trying to find an honest, yet age-appropriate, answer for my son's question for hours. It's perfectly acceptable to say to your kids, "Wow! I'm glad you asked me that, and I'd love to talk to you more about it. Can we wait until tonight when Mommy has a bit more time to talk and I promise we'll discuss it?" (Note: It's essential that you always come back to discuss it. Otherwise delaying is basically ignoring, and trust me: your kid hasn't forgotten the question.)

4. Tell your kids a lot of stuff.

Kids are curious. And that's why I try to tell my kids about whatever things are going on in the world. Tell them about storms and illnesses and politics and sports in an age-appropriate way so that when something new comes up, the first thing they think is, *Hmm. I'd better ask my mom about that, because she knows* everything *about everything.*

The Complimenting Balance Beam

I love inviting my brother-in-law Peter over to my house for dinner. Whatever I serve him—well, unless it's sprouted tofu with fish sauce—Peter rants and raves about how great it is. And eats every bite. And then asks for the recipe. I feel like the best chef in the world! And it's not just me and my cooking—Peter compliments his wife, my mom, his friends—everyone—diligently and beautifully. And he means every word he says. It's a great character trait he has. And—score for Peter—his well-placed and heartfelt compliments make me want to invite him over often. Plus, when he is coming over, I do my best to make recipes I know he'll like. His compliments inspire me to work harder for him.

On the other hand, inappropriate complimenting can actually damage kids. I read an article on Mr. Google that talked about how when kids are over-complimented in school—like when a teacher says, "Great job" when a student does average work—the kids stop trusting the teacher's words. I'm not sure if there's any research to prove this, but anecdotally, it makes sense. I mean, kids are smart. And if they're told they did great work when it's not great work, they're going to start catching on that perhaps their teacher or parents are just paying them lip service.

As parents we have to walk on a balance beam when it comes to complimenting. Fall off to one side and we're cold and uncaring—we fail to tell our kids when they're truly doing something great and encouraging their positive behaviors. But if we fall off to the other side, our words aren't genuine. And our kids quickly catch on that the things we're saying don't line up with the effort they're making. And that encourages less-than-great behavior and effort. So how do we walk the line—okay, more like *talk* the line—so we can compliment our kids in a way that's effective and best for their growth? Here are some ideas:

3 Habits of a Gold-Medal Complimenter

1. Compliment the behavior. Your kid is pretty amazing. But your kid didn't do anything to make himself smart or handsome or athletic. God did. And God deserves the glory for that. So, instead of complimenting your kid for his God-given talents, compliment him when he behaves in a way that honors God by being kind or honest or selfless or hardworking.
2. Limit praise. There's something to be said for choosing your battles when it comes to complimenting. So, just as you're not going to point out every not-so-great thing your kid does, you also don't have to point out every great thing your kid does. If you rave about how great an artist your kid is every time he draws a picture, well, you'll be doing a lot of raving. So, say you like it, and tack each picture on your already-full fridge, but save your praise for the times your kid does one of those rare, once-in-a-lifetime (okay, once-in-a-daytime) pieces.
3. Be genuine. My son Joey's scissor skills are, well, let's just say "choppy." And this lack of cutting expertise caused some

problems on some of his kindergarten work—something that was quite obvious when he brought home assignments. And so, when I looked at those assignments, I said things like, "I can see you're working on cutting" or, "I can tell you tried really hard on the coloring" or, "Wow! You're improving on your cutting." But never, "Great cutting, Joey." Because both Joey and I knew it wasn't great cutting.

Pretty Great Communicators Anonymous

I think it's become fairly apparent that, as great a communicator as I think I am, I still have some work to do. So I'll go ahead and update the name to Pretty Great Communicators Anonymous as I file for the patent. I wouldn't want to mislead anyone. Because, honestly, I think every mom could stand to learn a bit about how to communicate with our kids. With that in mind, I asked my mom to finish the chapter with a list of common phrases that moms say to their kids, and to use Scripture to rephrase those words so they will make a bigger impact. I love what she came up with—in fact, I printed this list and put it on my fridge and have already started using it to communicate with my kids. (If you want it, too, head to christianmamasguide.com and download a copy.)

. . . .

From the Principal's Office

Changing Your Words to Communicate Better
by Ellen Schuknecht

Every word you say to your kid helps shape him or her in some way. Here are some ideas on how you can use biblical principles to reshape your words in order to encourage your kids to seek Christ in everything they do.

Rather Than . . .	Try . . .
"Wow! You got an A."	"Your hard work really paid off. I'm proud that you persevered when things got tough." (Hebrews 12:1–3)
"You are such a good boy."	"I can see you are learning to be kind [patient, loving, self-controlled, etc.] like Jesus, who helps us be more like Him." (Galatians 5:22)
"You are the next American Idol."	"I love that God granted you the ability to bring honor to Him through your voice." (1 Peter 4:10)
"You ought to be ashamed of yourself. I don't ever want to see you do that again."	"Wow. You must be feeling really awful for what you did. Regardless, I love you and forgive you and am here to help you figure out what you need to do to make things right." (Psalm 86:5)
"You are special. There is no one like you."	"Just like the rest of us, you were created to reflect God's image in a unique way in serving others." (Genesis 1:27)
"You're such a brat."	"I am waiting for you to treat your brother thoughtfully." (Romans 12:10)
"Who are your friends?"	"How do they treat you?"
"How are you being a friend to others?"	"Who did you treat with kindness today?" (Proverbs 17:17)
"She is shy [or timid or sensitive]." (Using fragile words to describe your child.)	She is learning to be confident as the person God created her to become." "She is practicing speaking up for herself." (Using growth words to describe your child.) (2 Corinthians 12:9)
"You must be hungry [tired, sick] to be acting so rudely."	"Even if you are hungry, it is not an excuse to behave poorly. It's never right to do the wrong thing." (1 Timothy 4:12)
"You are awesome."	"Our awesome God is honored when you do excellent work." (Colossians 3:23)

TEN

The Christian Daddy's Guide to Starting School

What Dads Need to Know About Sending Their Kids out into the World

have a secret about dads—a secret my husband (and your husband) can never know. Okay, so I probably shouldn't be starting a chapter for dads with a secret I don't want dads to know, but seeing as how most men are efficient creatures and are probably already skimming to figure out when they'll get to the actual advice, I figure I'm pretty safe to talk about them behind their backs up here in the chapter intro. And now that I've babbled on and on for several sentences about how they are probably not reading this anyway, I figure my secret has been well protected. So here goes: dads are better at letting go than moms are.

Now, the reason dads can't ever know this is because they might get a complex. I mean, all it takes is a few words about them being "better" and we'll have a whole bunch of men strutting around, showing off their letting-go skills. It'd be downright annoying. Plus, I like to live in the world where I'm the one who gets complexes and my husband is the one who manages to calm me down with ice cream and back rubs. And so you can see how it just wouldn't work if he found out that I know he's a better letter-goer than I am.

Bottom line: your husband is probably actually pretty darn good at letting go. And to say more, he probably has some tricks up his sleeve about equipping your kid with The Fifteen Factors as well. And even if he hasn't sharpened up those skills just yet, I'm guessing that with a little practice, he could get really good at teaching your kid about things like courage and perseverance and work ethic and faith. But don't tell him that. Just set this book on his pillow with a bookmark on this page and let him find out for himself how other dads have managed to survive *and* love their kid's first school years.

The Christian Daddy's Guide to the First School Years

First, let's meet our panelists:

- ✐ *Troy* is my go-to panelist for The Christian Daddy's Guide—not only because he has three kids and thus, plenty of stories, but also because he'll do anything for a batch of my famous chocolate chip cookies. Even write stories for a Christian women's book.
- ✐ *Cameron* (my husband) is actually really good at teaching my kids about The Fifteen Factors. So good, in fact, that I often secretly take notes when he's talking to my kids so I can try the same strategies when he's not home.
- ✐ *John* has a first-grade daughter and a third-grade son—

which means he's an old hand at sending his kids off into the world. But he also just found out his wife is pregnant with (surprise!) an unexpected third child—which means he's been spending a lot of time reflecting on how to do it all over again.

Here's what they think you—and your husband—need to know.

John on Macho, Macho Men

Lesson #119: Being a wimp is okay . . .
except when it comes to haircuts.

My son is a total wimp. My wife is going to kill me for saying that out loud and in public, but he is. And I confess that his lack of courage drives the football-playing, motorcycle-riding, manly man in me absolutely crazy. My wife has tried to help me see the silver lining in his wimpiness—to see that his cautiousness will result in fewer trips to the emergency room and less worry for us as he goes through school. But I just see my son sitting at the top of a slide, crying as a growing line of impatient (yet courageous) children expands behind him. And it drives me absolutely nuts.

Nate is even a wimp when it comes to getting his hair cut. A haircut! For every other kid it's a snip here, a snip there, and done. But for Nate, it's an hour-long process where we have to reassure him (again) that the trimmer can't cut his skin and then twenty minutes of panicked flailing that results in a choppy, unkempt haircut that serves as a daily reminder of my son's lack of courage.

This is all very frustrating for me because—agree with me here, men—I want my kids to be courageous. I want them to be willing to try new things, to fight new battles, to stick up for what is right. And when I see my son doing the exact opposite, something in my heart wants to shake the fear out of him. But—and I'm sure you could guess this—courage (or lack thereof) is not what makes a man. God is. And I'm reminding myself that God made Nate with wonderful talents and gifts that make him who he is, regardless of how brave he is in the face of a big, scary bike (with training wheels) or a tiny baby goat at the petting zoo.

And so I'm learning to be patient with my son—wimpy as he is. Because I know that God is doing a good work in his heart. I've stopped pointing out the times he's being a wimp—I've found that only makes it worse. Instead, I've reminded him again and again what it means to be a man of God—strong, faithful, honest, and yes, even courageous.

Troy on Honesty

Lesson #435: It's always a good idea to spy on your kids.

I don't purposefully spy on my kids. Or at least I didn't until last week when I realized how beneficial it could be to show up at my kid's school at just the right moment. I happened to drop by my son's school during recess and walked out onto the playground just in time to see my son being pulled aside by a teacher. He didn't see me, so I watched from a distance as the teacher pulled him aside and had a lengthy conversation before sending him back to play with the other kids.

That evening I asked him what had happened on the playground that day. After pretending to give it some thought, he very confidently responded that nothing at all had happened on the playground. I pushed a little more—directly asking him if he had gotten into trouble with a teacher, and he looked at me with added resolve and firmly told me that no way, no how had he gotten into any trouble that day on the playground. The kid was lying through his teeth.

Of course I strung him along a bit longer, asking if he was absolutely, 100 percent sure that he hadn't gotten into any trouble at all that day. Finally, he broke. He slumped in his chair and asked me how I knew. And naturally, I told him that dads have their ways of knowing every little thing their kids do, so he should never, ever even think about trying to lie to me again. Okay, so I didn't say that. I told him it didn't matter how I knew, because the truth is that God sees everything, and He expects our hearts to be honest. And that's when the tears came.

I have to say that walking onto that campus and spying on my kid that day was a brilliant parenting move if I do say so myself. Because what started out as a little incident—Jude had gotten a little rough on the playground—resulted in Jude learning a whole lot about God's desire for complete truth in our lives. The conversation we had that night—about honesty and respect and forgiveness—was far deeper than I would've expected from a five-year-old. And Jude learned his lesson: daddy sees everything. His heavenly Daddy, at least.

John on Bossiness

Lesson #875: Your kid is not in charge
of you. At least, not yet.

"Daaaadddy, don't put my sandwich in the green container. I like it in the pink container. Oh, and cut the crusts off, would you?"

Sounds like a scene from a horror movie, doesn't it? Or the closest thing to it—a made-for-TV Disney movie. And yet, those are the exact words my six-year-old daughter said to me this morning. Only, with a screechy, whiny voice that made me not only want to throw that sandwich at her, but also to plug my ears and leave the room.

How does a six-year-old learn to talk like that? I'll tell you exactly how: she doesn't. My daughter was born bossy. Even when she was two, she had no problem telling me exactly what she thought I should be doing at any given moment. And as she's grown, it's gotten worse. It is really annoying for me, and I can only imagine how much more frustrating it is for her friends at school.

Recently, my wife and I decided to try a new tactic: we completely stopped asking her about who she played with or how she had fun at school. These questions seemed to feed her bossy, self-centeredness. Instead, we have been asking her questions like, "How were you a good friend at school today?" or, "What was one thing you did to make someone feel loved?" in hopes of helping her start thinking about what kind words and actions can mean to friendship. This is not the secret pill to fix her, I'm sure, but we have seen marked growth in her perspective. Let's hope it carries over to when I'm making her lunch, because frankly, I'm tired of being bossed around.

Cameron on Misbehavior at School

*Lesson #1234: Your kid isn't being ridiculous
on purpose. He was just made that way.*

My son Joey is the kind of kid who is so excited about everything he learns that he just can't help talking about it. And shouting about it. And dancing about it. And there are times when all that talking and shouting and dancing can be a bit disruptive in class. And those are the days when I get a call from the teacher to tell me that he's having one of his wild-and-crazy days.

I'm an assistant principal. I work in a school, and I know how disruptive misplaced exuberance can be to the learning environment. And so when I get those calls, it takes everything in me to keep from hopping in my car and driving down to Joey's school to teach him a lesson about how to behave in class. Because not only am I upset with Joey for being disruptive, but I'm also embarrassed that I can't seem to figure out a way to get a handle on my son's behavior. I know all the tricks! Yet none of them seem to work with my son.

I remember a day last year when we were driving home and I was just seething. Joey had done something small in class—knocked a kid's paper off of his desk or something like that—but I just couldn't figure out what it was going to take to teach Joey some impulse control. I mean, is it really that hard to listen to God's voice? I lost it and I snapped at Joey. I asked him why in the world he was acting that way at school. And he looked at me, wide-eyed, and said, "I just don't think, Daddy."

And it dawned on me: he wasn't purposefully being ridiculous;

he just wasn't thinking. And my yelling and ranting and lecturing and correcting weren't going to help him learn to think. He knows what's right and wrong. But in moments of weakness (or exuberance), he forgets everything he knows and does the wrong thing. So I'm trying a new strategy: I'm giving him thinking strategies.

So, for example, at home this morning, he was eating breakfast with his sister and reached out and snatched a blueberry off her plate. And instead of giving him the rundown about how we don't take food off other people's plate—something he already knows—I asked him what he could've done to help himself remember to keep his hands to himself. And he said, "I could probably stop and think before doing things." He came up with that all on his own. Smart kid, eh? Anyway, his new "stop and think" mantra won't solve all our problems, but it will at least get him started in working on self-control. At least I hope so.

John on Unsavory Characters

Lesson #1764: Even if you want to hop in your car and go strangle someone, you shouldn't.

My son, Nate, is in the third grade. Grade 3. Three years of schooling under his belt. He's nine. See a theme here? He is in no way old enough to be hearing about things like dating or sex or alcohol. And even if he were old enough, he should be hearing these things from me and not from the crazy, warped mind of a teacher who clearly shouldn't be teaching children.

Can you tell I'm a little worked up? Let me give you the backstory: my son came home the other day and said, "Mr. Hopkins thinks Ms. Jenkins is hot, hot, hot." I held my temper. At that point. I calmly asked Nate who Mr. Hopkins was (a PE teacher) and how Nate knew (he had been asked to bring a note to Mr. Hopkins's office from his teacher, and Mr. Hopkins had oh-so-maturely told my third grade son that he could tell his "hot" teacher that he'd see her that night over a bottle of wine.) And so, from that lovely snippet, Nate had ascertained that (a) it was okay to call a teacher hot, hot, hot, and (b) Mr. Hopkins and Ms. Jenkins drink wine together after school. He's in third grade. Did I mention that?

I was naturally furious. But I stayed calm enough to talk to Nate about how some teachers went on dates with each other after school and how, while it's not appropriate to call a teacher "hot," Mr. Hopkins was probably only saying it because he thought Ms. Jenkins was pretty. Nate and I talked about respect and dating and all sorts of other things. And it was a great conversation.

And as soon as it was over, I kissed Nate good night and went downstairs to plan my morning trip to the school, where I was going to give Mr. Hopkins plenty of pieces of my very angry mind so he could know that it is never, in no way, shape, or form, appropriate to talk to a nine-year-old that way. But my wife stopped me mid-rant.

"But aren't you glad you had that conversation with Nate?"

What? No! Of course I wasn't glad. Who wants to have a conversation like that with their kids? But then I thought about it. And that's exactly the kind of conversation I want to have with my kids. Nate asked me questions he would've never asked otherwise, and I told him things about my beliefs that I never would've said without a catalyst. We left the conversation with a stronger relationship.

Your kid is going to hear things in the world—whether he's in first grade or third grade or twelfth grade. He's going to encounter people who don't believe the same way you do. And while your gut reaction may be to be angry with these people for exposing your kid to "sin" or "corruption" or "worldly things," the truth is that these people are exposing your kid to opportunities to solidify his own faith. And to deepen his relationship with you.

I never went down to Nate's school the next day. I never told Mr. Hopkins that I knew what he said or mentioned to Nate's teacher, Ms. Jenkins, that he had been upset. Because I realized that I can't protect Nate from every wrong thing that he could hear, see, or feel. But I can prepare him to face those things with a courageous faith and a heart that truly seeks God.

*Lesson #2379: Your kid probably isn't ready for a
theological dissertation on the book of Ezekiel.*

I'm starting to learn that teaching theology to a five-year-old
is a lot like teaching my wife the mating habits of spiders. She just
doesn't seem to catch on about how cool it is. In fact, I'm starting to
think my son occasionally tunes me out when I read to him out of
Leviticus.

But the Bible—Deuteronomy chapter 6, to be exact—commands
parents to "impress" these words on the hearts of their children
(v. 7). Many translations actually use the words "teach them diligently" instead of "impress." I like *impress* or *inculcate* because
these words communicate the nature of how this diligent teaching should take place. Whoa! My seminary background took over
my keyboard for a second there. Back to reality: Teaching our kids
about God is not a onetime, major-teaching effort. It is not plugging
your kid into the right church once a week. It's showing them God
in everything you say and do and in who you are.

I have to go back to my seminary talk for a second, so hang with
me. The word *impress* is the same root word as *impressionism*.
In impressionistic painting, the artist made many small, seemingly insignificant dabs of paint on the canvas. No single dab was
a masterpiece, but the combination of all the brushstrokes created
beautiful art. And the word *inculcate* has Latin roots. The idea was a
repeated hammering onto metal in order to shape it. It is used these
days to speak of a teaching by persistent, repeated admonition.

If we are to diligently teach our kids about the things of God,
we must take advantage of all the little opportunities that present
themselves throughout the day. It is actually much easier because
you do not need to rely upon one amazing effort of instruction or
Bible reading, but rather many, frequent, little, seemingly insignificant efforts that will accumulate over time into a masterpiece or a
functional piece of metal that has been hammered into its proper

shape. To put it simply: show your kids who God is in every little thing you do.

The Christian Daddy's Guide to Big Kids

(For Those Daddies Who Only Have Time to Read One Page)

- Let God's love shine in everything you do.
- If there is ever an opportunity for you to go James Bond and spy on your kids, take it. And use it to your advantage.
- There's never really a good reason to give your kid a haircut. Long and shaggy is the new black.
- If your kid is whining at you about how you make her lunch, you could just stop making her lunch altogether. Cafeteria slop and yellow Jell-O it is!
- Reading to your kids from Leviticus is a great idea. Right up there with discussing things like forklift hydraulics, fancy TV remotes, deluxe wrench sets, and boxing stats during your next date night.
- Calling your kid a wimp will probably not make him more courageous. Throwing him into the lake, on the other hand, well, it's worth a try.
- The way your kid behaves doesn't reflect on you. Much, at least.
- The older your kid gets, the more fun it's going to be to talk to him. The more exasperating too.
- Every word you say is making a difference for your kid. So choose your words carefully, and sprinkle your conversations with grace and truth.

ELEVEN

When Things Don't Go "Right"

What to Do When Your Kid Struggles in School

'm going to slip on my serious hat for a few minutes so I can talk to you about academic struggles. Which means I'm not only going to have to avoid any urge to crack a potty joke—something that's tough for anyone who spends large amounts of time with the five-to-six-year-old crowd—but I'm also going to have to enlist the help of my mom, who has a much deeper understanding of how kids learn. Because this chapter is serious—if your kid is struggling in school, you are the first line of defense to get your kid the help he or she needs. And we want to help you help your kid.

You can probably already guess what I'm going to say, but I'll say it anyway just to make sure I make my point loud and clear: God created your kid with a unique learning personality. He also gave your kid unique, God-given skills, talents, and

121

abilities. Which means your kid may be one of those kids who is reading at a sixteenth-grade level in kindergarten. Or, he could be one of those kids who can't read at a kindergarten level in kindergarten.

Wherever your kid is on the continuum, one thing is certain: when it comes to academic struggles and learning disabilities, your job as a parent is to help your kid learn and grow. Notice I didn't say your job is to make sure your kid gets straight As or proper remediation. I said your job is to help him learn and grow. Which means that when your kid is struggling, you should absolutely do everything in your power to intervene, but not necessarily in the ways you might expect.

As my mom told me, probably the biggest misconception parents have is that learning disabilities and struggles are a bad thing. They assume that if their kids are labeled as "dyslexic" or "autistic" or "math-phobic," then they're destined to struggle in school and in life. But it's simply not true. God created your kid—and let me remind you again that He had a plan and a purpose as He knit together every detail—and that means even the so-called bad things were allowed with His ultimate plan in mind. Just remembering that God has a plan and a purpose for your kid in spite of his learning struggles can help you to better help your kid. It means instead of doing everything you can to try to "overcome" and "get past it," your focus shifts to doing everything you can to help your kid grow toward God's ultimate purpose for his life, which, by the way, is a saving faith and a heart that wants to serve Christ. So that reading assessment that has been your top priority for the last few weeks? It pales in comparison to your kid learning important Fifteen Factors skills, like empathy, persistence, courage, and work ethic.

My mom told me a story about a third-grade girl—we'll call her Sarah—who clearly struggled from day one in reading and writing. Her parents were desperate to help her, but they were also desperate to avoid a "label," so they called tutors and spent hours working with her at home and even made Sarah quit her beloved ballet classes so she could focus on reading. They did everything they could to help—except for the one thing they needed to do: get her tested for dyslexia.

After almost two years of an uphill battle, a teacher finally intervened and begged Sarah's parents to get her tested. And, lo and behold, it turns out she had a learning disability. Once she got "labeled," a whole world of opportunity for growth opened up for Sarah. Special strategies were employed, and therapists were called in. And most important, in retrospect, Sarah's parents realized that a "label" isn't always a bad thing. Instead, it was an opportunity for them to know how to help her. And, what's more, Sarah's so-called disability has proven to be a tool that God is using to help Sarah fulfill His purpose for her life and to grow in The Fifteen Factors. Which, in case you aren't catching on to my point here, is a great thing.

Sadly, there are times when all kids are going to struggle. And some kids will struggle when than others. As much as it pains us to watch our kids trudging uphill, we have to remind ourselves that God is always in control—and that He has an ultimate purpose for anything and everything that happens. With that in mind, I've quizzed my mom on the ins and outs of learning struggles so we can help you help your kid. So that he can thrive *because* of his learning struggles, and not in spite of them.

How Do I Know If There's a Problem?

Most kids—strike that; all kids—will struggle in some area in the course of their schooling. That's just part of learning. But you already figured that out in third grade, when your teacher wanted you to agree that half a pie and two-quarters of a cake were the same amount of dessert, regardless of the fact that the cake had a mile of pink frosting that clearly made it superior. Or maybe I was the only one who struggled with that. Certain concepts are just difficult for some kids—whether it's reading or writing or food-related fractions. And that's okay. It's part of the growing and learning process.

But for some kids, learning is more than hard. And these kids need special intervention and help. But how can we as parents know if our kids' struggles are just normal learning differences or something more?

My mom says that her first red flag that there might be a learning disability is when a parent or teacher says that a kid is lazy. She says she rarely sees a lazy five-year-old. Lazy teenagers, yes, but five-year-olds are still young and idealistic enough that they want to learn and grow. They're excited about stories and books and math manipulatives, and while some may not enjoy the day-to-day processes at school, most of them have an innate desire to learn and grow. And so, when she hears parents saying things like, "My kid just doesn't want to put in the work to learn to read" or, "He's lazy with his homework," the warning bells start to ring in her head.

When our kids start to struggle, our natural tendency as parents is to try to look for an easy fix. And blaming it on laziness is easy. But spend some time really observing your kid. Watch as you read stories to him or work on letters. And ask yourself if he's really being lazy, or if it's something else. Oftentimes when a kid seems lazy, what's really happening is that he's so overwhelmed that he shuts off his brain and stops trying. It's a defense mechanism, not laziness.

As a parent, you need to trust your gut. If you notice your kid not catching on to a specific concept or skill after reasonable teaching, then you are right to worry there's a problem and intervene. This doesn't mean you need to make a big production of it, but simply that you should take the next steps in order to help your kid.

Time-Out for Mom

For When Your Kid Is Struggling in School

"But blessed is the one who trusts in the Lord,
whose confidence is in him.
They will be like a tree planted by the water
that sends out its roots by the stream.
It does not fear when heat comes;
its leaves are always green.
It has no worries in a year of drought
and never fails to bear fruit." (Jeremiah 17:7–8)

Lord, I know that we all face trials as part of living in this world. Yet it's so hard for me to watch the tears stream down my kid's precious face! My heart sinks as he struggles. But he is not defeated! Help my kid to see himself as You see him, Lord, as a child with a purpose and a plan, who will bear true spiritual fruit when the time comes. Lord, give him confidence in the person You created him to be so that regardless of temporal struggles, he will be certain of Your life-changing grace today. Amen

Intervening for Your Kid

You're worried. Your husband is worried. Your cat's cousin's dog is worried. And it's time you slipped on that hot-pink supermommy-to-the-rescue cape and intervened to help your kid. But how? What can you do to make sure your kid gets the grease (figuratively) without turning him (and you) into an obnoxious, squeaky wheel? I polled my mom, as well as several of my friends who have dealt with learning struggles, to find out their best tips and ideas. Here's what they think you should do:

Tip #1: Include your kid in your intervention.

My mom told me about a family who desperately wanted to help their son, who struggled with a form of autism. They spent hours each week talking to therapists and teachers and specialists—but spent very little time talking to him. And as they valiantly fought behind the scenes to help their son, he shrank back, alone and seemingly uncared-for. While their intentions were good, they didn't involve him in the process, which made him feel isolated and as if his learning struggles were somehow his fault.

Throughout the entire learning process—and your kid's entire life—you should communicate with him first in a way that's developmentally appropriate. That means before you go to your kid's teacher, pull your kid aside and say, "I can tell this is really hard for you, and I want to try to figure out how to help you. I'm going to talk to your teacher to see if we can work together to find a solution." By including your kid in your intervention, you're showing him that you trust him enough to be your partner in the process.

Tip #2: Talk to your kid's teacher.

Your kid's teacher is probably your biggest ally in your quest to help your kid. Not only did she go to school for years to learn about learning disabilities and learning struggles, but she is also very invested in your kid's success. My mom says that the very first thing you should do is set up a conference with your kid's teacher to discuss your concerns. Chances are, your kid's teacher has already noticed the same thing and will have strategies in place to help. And if not, you can work together to find the resources you need to help your kid.

Tip #3: Check vision and hearing.

Before you even begin to consider learning disabilities, make an appointment to get your kid's hearing and vision screened. My mom says she can think of at least three or four instances each year where a teacher or parent is concerned about a kid's ability to learn, and it ends up being a simple vision or hearing problem that can easily be corrected with a pair of glasses or a hearing aid. Kids who can't see well or hear well can't learn well, and this is often the first—and only—thing a kid needs to be successful.

Tip #4: Go to an ophthalmologist.

If your kid passes a basic vision screening, the next thing you should do is make an appointment with an ophthalmologist to rule out more complex vision issues. Standard vision screenings—like the kind all kids get in public schools—evaluate only for distance visual acuity, but do not screen for how well the eyes focus up close or work together. Last year, after months of difficulty with reading, my friend Jen's second-grade son, Nate, went to an ophthalmologist on the advice of a reading specialist. The doctor found that Nate's eyes weren't focusing correctly, causing his eyes to cross and creating a strange double vision. It was almost impossible for him to see words on paper. With some corrective therapy with an occupational therapist, Nate is now reading at grade level.

Tip #5: Don't try everything; try the right thing.

My friend Megan told me that when her daughter Natasha started to struggle in school, her instant reaction was to try every possible strategy to "fix" Natasha's learning issues. She hired a private reading specialist to tutor Natasha, enrolled her in a specialized program for struggling kids, and bought expensive home materials and did them with her. And all those things can be good things—but they ended up making Natasha feel overwhelmed and overworked. Don't just throw "fixes" at the problem. Instead, work with your kid's teacher, doctor, or specialists to come up with a specific strategy for your kid—a strategy that has been proven to work for your kid's particular issues. And if that strategy doesn't work, try something else.

Tip #6: Don't be afraid of "alternative" solutions.

My friend told me the other day that she tried every imaginable solution—mediation, therapy, the works—to deal with her son's ADHD. So when a therapist suggested that she try combining short periods of concentration with breaks that involved heavy muscle exercise, she was skeptical. But she was also desperate. So she had her son work on his homework for ten minutes, and then go outside and do pull-ups on their backyard play set. She was shocked when his productivity increased significantly.

One huge caveat: alternative solutions are great when they involve simple fixes like the one I just described. But if an "alternative" solution is invasive—like something that calls for an extreme change in diet, herbal medications, or therapy that's going to involve a large amount of time or money—you should be very wary. I'm not saying those things can't or won't work, but simply that intense or invasive therapy should always be carefully considered with the help of your kid's teacher and doctor.

Tip #7: Be patient in the process.

There will probably not be a quick fix or easy solution to your kid's learning difficulties. It may take years of struggle, and you may at times feel hopeless and desperate and alone. But your desperation to find a fix can make your kid feel equally desperate—and as if there is something wrong with him. Instead, be patient as things get figured out. Be willing to listen as your kid and teachers share progress as well as issues. And most important, stand firmly in your kid's camp in a way that shows him you love him exactly how God made him.

Tip #8: Recognize that there may not be a solution.

There's not a magic pill for every problem in life. Which means your kid may struggle with reading or math or social learning for his entire life. And while I firmly believe you should do everything you can to help your kid overcome difficulties, I also want to encourage you to recognize that there may not be a perfect solution. And that doesn't mean that God made a mistake.

Who knows what God has in store for your kid? And who knows how God is using these struggles to grow your kid into the person He wants him to be. With that in mind, there are times when it's okay to simply embrace the learning process and recognize that while there may not be a way to help your kid be top of his class academically, there are lots of other incredible ways God gifted your child. And that's what you can focus on.

Taking Off My Serious Hat

Before I slip off my serious hat, I want to remind you that I'm not an expert when it comes to learning struggles. As such, I can't speak to the best ways to help a struggling kid. I did talk to several people in the course of writing this chapter—and did my best to give you tried-and-true advice and been-there, done-that tips. But that's not enough! If you are worried about your kid, seek the help of a teacher or doctor or therapist who can help. I can guarantee that they certainly know a lot more about how to help than I do. (And they probably know your kid better too!)

And now the somber, gray, serious hat is coming off, and a bright, sparkly, glittery hat is being placed on my head. Because next up we're talking about kids' misbehavior. And let's just say the conversation involves glitter glue, a complicated two-part behavior chart, and my wanting to disown my kid from time to time.

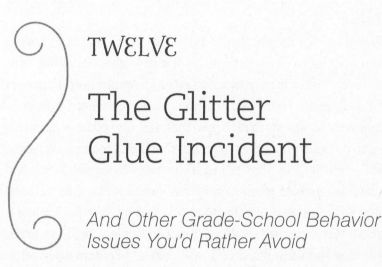

TWELVE

The Glitter Glue Incident

And Other Grade-School Behavior Issues You'd Rather Avoid

My son Joey is a sand partier. Draw a figurative line in the sand and tell him not to cross it, and he's not only going to sprint as fast as he can to the other side, but he's going to bring all his friends with him and throw a party in the forbidden territory. So I knew when I sent him off to school that I was going to probably get some "Joey was chatty in class" calls and perhaps the occasional "Joey ran through the hall" notes. I even braced myself for the dreaded "Joey knocked someone over on the playground" message. But I have to admit that in my wildest dreams, I never expected the glitter glue pink slip.

To be fair, Joey claims he was trying to help his friend Sarah with her hairdo. Apparently she was trying to be super-girl and needed a way to permanently keep her hair pink and sparkly so she could, you know, look the supergirl part. So Joey helped her out. And squirted an entire tube of (permanent) pink glitter glue into her long, wavy hair. And—shockingly—Sarah and her parents didn't think Joey's method was quite as brilliant as Joey thought it was.

I do feel bad for Sarah. Really, I do. I mean, it must have been a nightmare trying to comb little globs of glitter glue out of her hair. But you have to allow me a moment of self-indulgence here: I also feel bad for me! Because I had to go to a crazy parent-teacher conference and explain to the assistant principal that, yes, my son does know it's not nice to put glue in people's hair, and then I had to keep a straight face while telling Joey that the sparkly green (washable) hair dye that I keep in the bathroom is our little secret and not something he should be trying to replicate at school. And by the time I made it through all forty minutes of glitter-induced crisis, I needed a good, strong mocha and a few hours on Pinterest just to regain my sanity.

My saving grace as I dealt with what I now oh-so-affectionately call "the Glitter Glue Incident" was the fact that I knew my redemption was coming in the form of a little towheaded girl in hot-pink boots. My daughter, Kate, is far from a sand partier. Kate's the type of kid who stands at least ten feet back from that imaginary line in the sand just to make sure she doesn't even get close to breaking a rule. She's sugary sweet, and I knew without a doubt that she would be the girl who stayed in at recess to help her teacher alphabetize the glitter glue—not the one to squirt it on other kids.

But even my saving grace has since disappointed me on that front. Behavior problems at school are very rare with her, thank goodness, but I've heard the occasional "Kate was chatty" report and even once a "Kate had to be put in time-out for messing with her friends during story time" note. And she's my "good" one! I don't even want to begin to imagine what I will hear when my tough-and-tumble baby, Will, reaches school.

But I digress. My point in telling you about Joey's—let's just call it "creative"—behavior at school is to make sure I have lots of public fodder with which to embarrass them into behaving when they're in high school and the stakes are higher. Oh, and I also want to reassure you that when you face the occasional behavior trial—and you will—it doesn't mean there is something wrong with your kid. Kids—like adults—have the occasional bad day. And those bad days sometimes lead to meltdowns. And while it tends to be pretty embarrassing when it happens—for you, not your kid—it's also almost always survivable. As long as you have a good sense of humor and an emergency supply of good chocolate.

I can't even begin to get deeply involved in the psychology of school behavior—mostly because I'm not a psychologist, but also because that's a book unto itself. But I do want to spend this chapter sharing a few things I've learned about school behavior so you can get yourself prepared for your own glitter glue incident. Or soccer ball incident. Or crayon-in-the-cafeteria incident. Because trust me, my friend: it's coming. Ready or not, it's coming.

10 Things That Could (Okay, Will) Cause Your Kid to Melt Down at School

1. His friend's library book is bigger than his.
2. His friend's library book is longer than his.
3. His friend got to sit in the red chair in the library, and he had to sit in the blue chair, and he had just decided on the way to the library that his favorite color was now red. (And why can't the librarian keep up with these things?)
4. A grape in his lunch got squished.
5. His toe got squished as he tried to throw away the squished grape in his lunch.
6. His friends wanted to play soccer on the playground, but Sam said he had to be on the punting team instead of the batting team, and that wasn't fair because last time Sam got to be the point guard.

7. His reading book was too hard.
8. His reading book was too easy.
9. He felt like having a meltdown.
10. He felt that today was the day he really didn't want to have a meltdown but had a meltdown anyway because he was thinking so hard about not having one.

· ·

Time-Out for Mom

For When Your Kid Is Struggling with Misbehavior

"But the fruit of the Spirit is love, joy, peace, forbearance, kindness, goodness, faithfulness, gentleness and self-control. Against such things there is no law. Those who belong to Christ Jesus have crucified the flesh with its passions and desires. Since we live by the Spirit, let us keep in step with the Spirit." (Galatians 5:22–25)

Lord Jesus, my kid is still learning and growing in You—and I know that—but it's so hard to watch him struggle to do the right thing. Fill him with Your Spirit so he can walk in love, joy, peace, forbearance, kindness, goodness, gentleness, and self-control. Because like me, he can't do it without You. Show him who You are today, Lord, and fill his heart with You so that he is able to make good choices that benefit everyone. Amen.

· ·

Dealing with School Misbehavior

At Joey's school, the teachers use a daily behavior log. It's very complicated—and it involves quite a bit of math and numbers—so from day one, I knew it was going to be my nemesis. Basically, there's a chart in the front of a little folder in his backpack that gets marked with a code—a code!—every day. If everything is A-OK, he gets a 1 in the box. A 2 means he had a warning or two. A 3 means time-out and a call home from the teacher. I don't even want to begin to contemplate what a 4 means because—thank goodness—so far we haven't dealt with that.

But that's not all. There are also letter codes. So "A" means "respect" and "B" means "body control," and so on. So if Joey comes home with a 2A in his folder, I know he got a few warnings through-out the day about showing respect. If he comes home with a 3BCQ, I know we're facing another glitter glue incident.

If you understand anything about me from reading this book thus far, I think it's pretty obvious how I feel about the behavior chart system. It's a very necessary evil. No offense to the teachers—I adore them and I totally get that they simply don't have time to write flowery notes home about all twenty-plus kids in their classes every day. But I *dread* opening Joey's backpack every single day because I know that I'm not only facing crazy, mathematical computations, but also the potential that my son did something mortifying at school.

After a few weeks of kindergarten, I reached a point where I was more scared of Joey's school folder than I was of the candy aisle at Target. I couldn't handle the pressure of looking and calculating and deciding what to do, what to buy. I mean, how to respond. And—in case it hasn't become obvious as you've read this book—I'm not good with stress. Especially stress that involves things like num-bers and codes and my kid squirting glue at other kids. So I booked a massage and a mani-pedi and made an inner vow to never look at the chart again.

Kidding! I called my mom.

And since I'm the sharing type—well, as long as it doesn't involve chocolate—I'll share her how-to-deal-with-misbehavior-at-school expertise with you. Right here, right now. So that you won't have to go into panic every time you catch a glimpse of your kid's take-home folder or see your teacher's number on your caller ID. Here's what I've learned—both from my mom and from my own experience.

1. It's probably not that big a deal.

First of all, let me make it super clear that I'm not minimizing the importance of good behavior at school. I know that teachers are dealing with twenty (plus) students, and one kid causing a distraction can cause the entire classroom to fall apart. It's super important that we teach our kids to be respectful, obedient, and attentive in the classroom. But—and this little *but* is the reason I've kept my sanity the last few years—the little blips on your kids' behavior charts are probably not that big a deal.

Yes, that's right. It is not the end of the world if your kid has a chatty day or gets so excited to get to gym class that he runs through the hallway, knocking down a poster in the process. Sure, you should address these minor incidents, but unless you're seeing a major pattern of bad behavior—or your kid does something absolutely ridiculous that requires your attention—you are pretty safe to assume there isn't a major issue.

2. Have a prepackaged response.

Part of the reason Joey's behavior chart was stressing me (and him) out was that I felt as if I had to do something to respond to it every single day. On the good days I felt I needed to have some sort of reward. On the bad days I felt I needed to discipline him. But Joey's teacher was simply communicating with me what had happened—and oftentimes, a simple acknowledgment was the only warranted response. So I talked to my mom, and we came up with a strategy. On good days I simply acknowledge the day—saying something like, "Wow, Joey! I can tell you had a great day today. What did you like about it?" On those level-2 days, when he gets warnings, I simply ask him what happened and how he could do better next time. Because the truth is that the teacher has already probably done enough to deal with minor incidents. And only when he gets a 3—which means the teacher had to warn him several times—do we go farther than that.

3. Don't overdo the discipline.

After the glitter glue incident, I was tempted to lay the punishment on thick with Joey—you know, to help him remember that in our house, we never (ever, ever, ever) act that way at school. But my mom reminded me that he had certainly already had plenty of consequences at school. And that over-disciplining would only frustrate him and make him feel that there had been an injustice. So, that night, we had him write an apology note to both little Sarah and his teacher, and then we left it at that. (And, by the by, he has not used any sort of glue on anything other than paper since. Score!)

4. Listen to your child.

A few weeks ago, Kate had a rough afternoon at school. Her teacher said she seemed grumpy and short and wasn't able to focus. I asked her what happened, because she rarely has rough afternoons, and lo and behold: she explained that her sandwich had dropped on the floor during lunch. And so, she'd hardly eaten anything. By mid-afternoon, she was not only hungry, but grumpy as well. While this doesn't excuse her behavior, it at least helped me get a picture in my mind about what had happened.

5. But also listen to your kid's teacher.

I can tell you with (almost) absolute certainty that (a) your kid's teacher isn't scheming against your kid, and (b) your kid's teacher probably has better perspective on the situation than your kid does. This isn't to say you shouldn't listen to your kid—you should always allow him the space to express his feelings in regard to any situation. But you should also take everything your kid says with a massive grain of salt and remember that your kid's teacher is doing his or her best to manage a large group of kids.

6. Be clear and consistent.

Be very clear with your kid about the expectations for behavior that you have set for your family. Even on the days when you just want to curl up on the couch and ignore the minor things, make it very clear that you expect honesty, integrity, respect, and so on.

7. Make your kid ponder his predicament more than you do.

It's easy for me as a mom to want to fix things for my kids. So when I hear about a misbehavior or problem, my first instinct is to tell them how to solve the problem. And to help them fix it. I probably don't have to tell you this, because you're a smart mama, and you probably already know this—but that doesn't help them. It teaches them not to solve their own problems. So instead of telling your kid what to do, ask him what he's going to do to solve the issue he has created. And then give him the space to come up with his own solutions. (Note: Your kid's solution may not be the same as your solution, and that's okay. The point is that he solves the problem, not that he solves the problem the way you would've.)

8. Don't be afraid to intervene in a big way for big issues.

Not all issues are small issues. They're not even all medium-sized issues like the glitter glue incident. And I'd be remiss if I didn't address the fact that at some point you may face a major behavioral issue with your kid. Because even good kids do bad things sometimes. And in these cases, it's your job to intervene in a big way. I won't go into specifics, but I know of a situation where a kid was biting other kids so hard he was drawing blood. And his mom stepped in and took control. She not only found a therapist to help deal with the biting, but she also headed to the school each day during recess (with the school's permission) to be on standby in case her kid started to bite. Her intervention not only saved her kid—he's grown and changed so much—but also made me respect her so much as a mom. Because regardless of what her kid was doing, he knew that he had a mom who cared enough to give him her best.

From the Principal's Office

How to Intervene When Your Kid Misbehaves
by Ellen Schuknecht

As a school administrator, I get visits on an almost daily basis from frustrated parents who aren't sure how to intervene on behavior issues. And I'm so glad they come to me! It shows they care, and I am often able to help them get perspective on the issue so that they can help their kids and their kids' teachers in a way that's productive and not destructive. Here are the tips I typically give them:

1. Accept the fact that your child will make mistakes and is on a learning journey. This learning journey includes social and emotional growth, which comes by way of social and emotional mess-ups. No child is by nature so good that he won't try out some pretty ugly actions. Accept it and move on.

2. Pray. Go to God before you go to others. Be your child's prayer warrior. The things you worry about today will change, and new things to worry about will appear tomorrow. He is growing and changing and learning, and prayer is the most important action you can do on his behalf.

3. Don't make quick decisions. Kids are very good at sharing only what supports their causes, and they learn to selectively "forget" details that don't. Often you will only hear issues from your child's perspective, so don't make decisions or send communications before getting all the details. In other words, never call your kid's teacher or another parent when you are emotionally upset. You will likely regret your overreaction when you calm down.

4. Listen to the teacher, and don't get defensive. Allow your kid's teacher to share both the good and the bad about your child. The truth is, the best teachers are the ones who are willing to help your kid stretch and grow. As hard as it is to hear tough

things about your child, it's equally difficult for a teacher to share tough things. With a teachable heart, be open to honest discussion so that you put together the best plan for growth.

5. Ask the teacher what she thinks you should do. Together you can come up with a strategy that will not only help your kid grow, but will also help you best support the teacher.

6. Be calm. Keep your emotions in check, especially the angry ones and the worry ones. Strong-willed children are often motivated by "out-of-control" moms and try out bad behavior just to get a reaction.

7. Expect your kid to seek forgiveness for his or her misdeeds. Have your child write a note of apology to a teacher for acting out in class. Expect him to talk to his friends and seek forgiveness for mean actions and to ask forgiveness from adults he has disrespected.

Analyzing Strength-Weakness Combos

Of course, even after you respond to your kid's misbehavior in an entirely appropriate and effective manner (as I always do—ha!), it's still important to consider the sources of the misbehavior so you can help your kid grow in The Fifteen Factors.

Each of my kids has unique strengths and talents—strengths and talents that make them the wonderful and fantastic people that God made them to be. But I've noticed that it's not my kids' faults that stand in the way of their personal growth; instead, it's the weaknesses that are associated with their strengths that cause trouble. Let me explain. Joey is very athletic—a good thing—but it also leads to competitiveness and overactivity in class. Likewise, Kate is very creative—she could sit and draw or write all day—but in a classroom situation, that manifests itself as flightiness and inattention. In other words, their upsides have related downsides. I'm learning to identify these strength-weakness pairings in my kids so I can guide them as they learn and grow.

Because considering these strength-weakness pairings has

helped me so much, I asked my mom to talk me through the most common strength-weakness combos that she sees in kids, and to give some tips on how parents can help their kids overcome their weaknesses to become the people that God created them to be.

Common Strength-and-Weakness Combos

1. Creative–Inattentive

As I've already said, my daughter, Kate, is a creative-inattentive. She lives in a constant state of creativity—whether it's writing a song in her head or imagining how she could repaint her bedroom. But she is also very flighty—she could daydream away the day.

Help your kid by: focusing on growing self-control by redirecting him to the task at hand—even if it means nagging (I mean, reminding) over and over.

2. Perfectionistic–Risk Averse

A few weeks ago, Joey had to do a reading assessment at school. This assessment didn't matter—his score had no bearing on his grade or his future or anything of the sort. It was simply a way for the teacher to gauge his strengths and weaknesses when it came to reading. But about halfway through the assessment, Joey stumbled on one word—one word—and completely shut down. He later told me that once he missed that word, he assumed he had failed, so he quit trying.

Help your kid by: teaching him to see mistakes and failures as opportunities to learn and get better so he is able to enjoy the learning process. Teach him the difference between excellence (which is attainable) and perfection (which isn't).

3. Driven–Bossy

I'm sure we all remember the know-it-all on the playground from grade school. Unless, of course, you were that person. I tended to be a bit bossy when I was a kid—I knew what I wanted, and I (thought I) knew how to get it, so I didn't hesitate to tell the other kids exactly what they should do. I was only helping them, of course.

Help your kid by: constantly reminding him—both in words and in action—that other people may have different ideas or do things differently, but that doesn't mean they're wrong.

4. Detailed–Inflexible

My nephew Jude is very detail-oriented. For example, when reading him a story, he'll notice every little picture, word, and nuance in the story. And this is a great thing when it comes to learning. But it also leads to inflexibility when it comes to behavior. I'm sure you can imagine what happens when you skip a word when reading to him or when an assignment hits a road bump.

Help your kid by: teaching him to relax his standards a bit by helping point out the things that do matter in any given situation and then pointing out the things that don't matter.

5. Competitive–Poor Sportsmanship

I'm not trying to call out my nieces and nephews here—I promise—but they'll thank me for it later when the whole world knows them as the "competitive one" or the "creative one." My sweet niece Haddie is very competitive. So last week, when she got a bike and was learning to ride it, it drove her crazy that she wasn't able to keep up with my kids, who had been riding bikes for years. After a short but frustrating ride, she stopped, hopped off the bike, and declared she was never riding again. And proceeded to walk next to her bike all the way home.

Help your kid by: giving him opportunities in which he will lose—yes, this is your chance to finally win in UNO—so he can learn how to lose graciously and pick up some humility along the way.

6. Relational–Easily Influenced

Kate—my creative one—is also a very relational kid. Everyone is her best friend, and she'll do whatever it takes to keep it that way. Just last week she got a prize from her teacher for memorizing and reciting a memory verse. She had worked so hard and was so proud of the little trinket she had picked out of the box. She talked about it all the way home, and anxiously carried it to show her big brother when we went to pick him up from school. Joey told her it was cool. And Kate's immediate response was to hand him her hard-earned prize and tell him it was a present. Then she burst into tears. When I asked her why she gave away her prized possession to her brother when she clearly didn't want to, she told me that she wanted Joey to be happy with her. She was so anxious to please others that she's easily swayed to do what she thinks other people want her to do.

Help your kid by: asking him what he thinks or feels before reacting, so he can learn to consider his own thoughts, feelings, and values when making decisions.

7. Leader–Bully

I don't want to make light of bullying, as it's a very serious issue, but I also want to point out that kids with strong leadership skills have the ability to influence other kids, which at times can manifest itself as bullying. Being a leader is a great characteristic—and you should do whatever you can to hone your kid's leadership skills—but if you notice that your kid is so bent on getting his own way that he's willing to hurt others in order to get it, you need to take action and intervene right away.

Help your kid by: understanding the effective leaders also have to learn to follow. Put your kid in situations—athletic teams, clubs—where he won't be the coach or leader so he can learn to take direction from others and become sensitive to their feelings and needs.

8. Thoughtful–Sensitive

Thoughtful children are often intuitive and make connections that show maturity beyond their years. But my mom said she also notices that thoughtful kids often overanalyze every word said to them, causing them to grow unrealistically fearful and concerned about how others perceive them.

Help your kid by: stopping any overanalytical thought patterns—especially ones that are overly sensitive—by redirecting to feelings words. Ask how other kids' words make her feel and whether she thinks her feelings could've been influenced by anything unrealistic.

The Aftermath

This has been a heavy chapter, hasn't it? Or maybe you've been all light and airy because my kid is the one getting those 3QRDs while your kid sits quietly and does his work. Regardless, I don't want to leave you on such a heavy note. And so I'll tell you what I've reminded myself of often during those dark moments when I want to scream in frustration at my sand-partier, Joey. I remind myself that it's actually kind of funny if you look at the big picture. Yes—even the glitter glue will be funny someday. And just to prove my point, I've jotted down a few of the things I've heard come out of my mouth as of late. Go ahead. Laugh at my expense.

7 Things I Never Thought I'd Hear Myself Say (Out Loud, at Least)

1. "If you hadn't put your snack on top of your homework, and then left it on the floor, the dog wouldn't have eaten it."
2. "Let's review: your unfinished tuna salad sandwich goes back into your lunch box to save for later. *Not* in your pocket."
3. "So what you're saying is that this all happened because you were pretending you were living in a video game and your friend Johnny had the controller? Finally something that makes sense."

4. "What do you mean you need me to come to school to clean the glue globs off your desk? Don't you know how to use a paper towel? Never mind. Don't answer that."

5. "Target is closed at 4:46 a.m. Why, again, do you need Silly String and a bag of Tootsie Pops for school today?"

6. "Pirate talk is for the dinner table, *not* your oral reading assessment."

7. "No, babies are not made when mommy and daddy get mad at each other. Wait! Who told you that?"

THIRTEEN

Michael Phelps Was Born Swimming

And Other Urban Legends About Talented Kids

have a story for you. And I'm 99.8 percent positive it is at least 1 percent true. And I never lie about stats. So here goes:

Once upon a time, in a faraway land, there was a woman named Debbie. Debbie was pregnant. One day Debbie was swimming and she felt a contraction. But since she already had two daughters, she assumed it was a Braxton Hicks contraction and kept swimming. The contractions kept coming, but Debbie kept on swimming. And suddenly, without any warning, her little boy popped out. But instead of sinking, he started swimming, all on his own. And that little boy was Michael Phelps—the man who went on to win twenty-two Olympic swimming medals.

Now, you may read that story and think it's a thinly veiled attempt by the League of Infant Athletes to recruit babies for their summer camp programs, but I want to go on the record as saying that it's—*gasp*!—a silly urban legend. I looked it up on Snopes.com. Well, that and I have enough experience with newborn babies to know that they usually can't do much other than poop and sleep for the first several months of life.

The only reason I'm spreading totally untrue rumors about Michael Phelps is to prove a point: it's easy to start to feel as though you're relegating your kid to a life on the sidelines if you don't sign him up for football camp or voice lessons before your second prenatal appointment. And that's just not true. I asked Mr. Google, and Michael Phelps didn't start swimming until he was *seven*. And—get this—many professional athletes and artists and musicians didn't spend their entire childhood years in the pool or on the field or in the studio. They had normal childhoods. And participated in a large range of activities.

That said, sports and other lessons can be a lot of fun for kids—some of my best memories as a kid involved running on the track team (I know: I had a warped sense of fun) and taking art lessons. And I want my kids to have those experiences. I want them to know what it means to play on a team or dance in a performance or display their masterpieces for all to see. It's a quintessential part of childhood. And I'm guessing most moms reading this want their kids to have similar experiences.

The world of extracurriculars involves a tricky balance between allowing our kids to experience life, and keeping ourselves from having an embarrassing televised conversation with Dr. Phil during his pageant mom special. And so, to help you find this balance, I've put together a list of the top eight urban legends involving kids' sports and activities so you can figure out the truth—and then get on with your sports-loving, art-making lives in a way that's a little bit more . . . sane.

Urban Mom Legend #1:Extracurricular activities are bad for kids' creativity and stress levels.

The Facts: There was a rumor—okay, an urban legend—going around a few years ago that kids should have freedom to learn and grow by gamboling aimlessly through fields of wildflowers and creating their own games using matchbook boxes and pinecones. This same legend said kids' creativity and drive could be destroyed by structured activities, like lessons, leagues, and teams. One mom friend of mine even went as far as to tell me that "un-activitying" is a way to allow our kids to learn and grow in the way that they were created—independently and freely.

This sounds like a nice idea in theory—and trust me: if I could avoid going to football practice every Thursday afternoon in 103-degree weather, I would—but I just don't buy it. Because I've seen so much growth and enjoyment in my kids when they've participated in organized extracurricular activities. And through sports and lessons, I've seen my kids' self-discipline, work ethic, courage, and perseverance grow by leaps and bounds.

Now, I'm not telling you to sign your kids up for sixteen activities and athletic clinics each weekend—see Urban Legend #2—but I do think that allowing our kids the opportunity to participate in activities is a great way to help them learn and grow at a time when they are still exploring who they are and what they enjoy. That and it gives you the opportunity to put those awesome baking skills to use for the team bake sale.

Savvy Mom Takeaways

- Ask your kids what activities they are interested in, and do your best to allow them the chance to participate.
- Don't be afraid to improvise. If there's no soccer league in

your town, pick up a soccer ball and meet a few friends at
the park for an impromptu pickup game.

- ∽ Don't sign up for a lifetime of karate lessons. Sign up for a
two-month trial and then reassess to see if your kid is still
enjoying it.

Urban Mom Legend #2: Busy kids are happy kids.

The Facts: I know I just told you that extracurricular activities
are good for kids—and they are. But busyness is not good for kids.
And when extracurricular activities take up every moment of free
time our kids have, they become a hindrance instead of a help. And
so, if you're finding yourself eating McNuggets in the minivan for
dinner more often than not, then you may want to cut back on the
activities.

I realized that I tend to be a busy-aholic after reading my friend
Joanne Kraft's book, *Just Too Busy*. Before my busyness break-
through, I actually used to live by the motto that busyness was
next to happiness—especially when my kids were toddlers and
their idea of a good time involved emptying my expensive shampoo
bottles onto the shower floor. So, to save my house and my sanity, I
signed them up for every kiddie-and-me class known to man. And
guess what? My sanity just got more frazzled as I tried to remember
whether Monday was Jumbo-Gym day or Kid-Cook-O-Rama day.

Joanne actually took her family on a "radical sabbatical," where
she made her kids cut out every activity in their schedules and
spend an entire year just being a family. Eating together. Playing
together. Doing everything together. And, although I'm not sure I'm
ready to go that far (um, that would mean no Starbucks runs during
soccer practice), I do see that Joanne has a point. Because despite
my earlier point that extracurricular activities do a lot for our kids,
by signing our kids up for every lesson, team, and activity we can

jam into their already tight schedules, we're just setting them up for a pre-adulthood meltdown.

Savvy Mom Takeaways

- ᕙ Sign your kids up for one activity at a time—soccer in the fall, gymnastics in the spring.
- ᕙ Leave plenty of time each week free.
- ᕙ Work family time into your schedule. Reserve Saturday afternoons for a family outing or Friday nights for game night.

Urban Mom Legend #3: Kids know from an early age what they want to be when they grow up.

The Facts: Joey wants to be a football player when he grows up. So, naturally, we do what we can to help him work toward his goal. We signed him up for neighborhood league flag football last year (where he's learned lots of football-esque skills, like how to run the correct way when scoring a touchdown and how to squirt water on his head from a bottle without getting his coach wet). We (okay, Cameron and Joey) toss the old pigskin around in the afternoons. And every Saturday in September, I whip up a batch of queso and we don our Longhorn gear so we can watch the big game. Because Joey loves football. And if that's what he wants to do with his life, well, then we're going to do our part to help him be what he wants to be. Within reason. And as long as it involves him wearing burnt orange. I'm kidding. Sort of.

Kate wants to be a fairy when she grows up. Which—by the by—is a bit harder to support than football. There just isn't a fairy league in town, and even if there were, I'm not sure what fairies exactly do other than sparkle and flitter—two skills that Kate already has down pat.

Either way, I have the feeling that neither of them are 100 percent decided on their future career paths. And who is at the tender age of six? I've changed my mind about what I want to be when I grow up at least six times—and that's just since I turned thirty-three. And with that in mind, I can cheer Joey on from the sidelines (or Kate on from the fairy field or wherever the local fairies do their work), but I'm not going to invest my entire life (or theirs) on their current dreams du jour.

Savvy Mom Takeaways

- Add some variety to your kid's life. Even if he loves soccer more than anything, mix things up with an art camp or piano lessons.
- Don't dedicate massive amounts of time to any one thing. Let your kid just be a kid sometimes—even if you're certain you've discovered the next all-around gold medalist.
- Even if your kid wants to be a fairy, you shouldn't take out a second mortgage to pay for a wing transplant.

Urban Mom Legend #4: If your kid has a God-given talent, then you should do whatever it takes to hone that talent. For God's kingdom, of course.

It's easy to get caught up in our kids' talents and start believing they're destined for stardom. Take Joey, for example. In his first football game when he was five, he got the ball and immediately ran for a runaway touchdown. With visions of the Superdome and a big college scholarship dancing through my head, I turned to high-five the other parents. And that was when I noticed that no one else seemed to be cheering. Turns out there's a rule in football that the other team gets points if you run backward and score a goal in their end zone. Who knew?

The point is that your kid certainly has God-given talents. And honing those God-given gifts is part of helping your kid grow up to be the person God created him to be. But your kid's natural abilities are not who your kid is. And as much fun as it is to start dreaming of your kid wearing the burnt orange and white (or whatever lowlier color you'd like him to wear), his heart, his soul, and his relationship with Christ should always take a precedent.

Savvy Mom Takeaways

- Praise your kid for hard work, good sportsmanship, and a positive attitude instead of for his or her natural talent.
- Cheer for your kid's team, not just your kid.
- If you ever start to worry that sports (or art or theater or music) are standing in the way of your kid's spiritual growth, don't be afraid to put the extracurriculars aside for a season. Or forever.

Urban Mom Legend #5: You must document every move your kid makes for future college recruiters.

The Facts: I've been known to take my fair share of pictures and videos of my kids in action. I've also been known to post my fair share of action shots on Facebook—because I know how much people l-o-v-e to see frame-by-frame videos of my kids doing ballet. But I'm starting to realize that my vigilant documentation is actually causing me to miss precious moments of actually *seeing* my kids perform. And it turns out college recruiters tend to only watch film from upper-level high school kids. Apparently they don't go back to first grade when assessing a kid's athletic potential.

- Spend more time watching the game than photographing the game.
- Bring your camera to one or two games or performances and get some great pictures that you can use at your kid's graduation. But then leave your camera at home.
- Don't even think about future college recruiting or sending the video in to *American Idol* until your kid is at least sixteen.

Urban Mom Legend #6: You paid a lot to get your kid in the team/league/club, so you'd better get your money's worth.

The Facts: I have drilled it into your head over and over throughout this book that your kid's heart is more important than your kid's success. And this is especially true when it comes to extracurriculars. Because I've seen many parents—myself included—get caught up in the fact that they've sacrificed so much for their kids' passions that they make their kids' activities a priority over their kids' hearts.

Back in my days as a high school teacher, I had a kid in my class (we'll call him Mike) who was a super-talented football player. Mike was being heavily recruited by a Division I school—and rumor had it that he was going to get a big scholarship to play. But there was one small problem: Mike was failing my class because he had skipped a test day to hang out with friends. And if he didn't manage a passing grade by the end of the week, district policy said he couldn't play the remainder of the football season. Which meant his scholarship would disappear, along with any hopes he had of going to college.

This did not make his mama happy.

I think a lot of moms would've come to me and begged me to change his grade—to bump him up so he could play and fulfill his dream. But not Mike's mama. She came to me with Mike in tow and told me that her expectation for her son was that he work hard at everything he did. And that meant he was going to find a way to make up for skipping class and failing or she would personally see to it that he was kicked off the football team. Because she'd rather raise a son with a strong work ethic than raise a lazy son who got a college scholarship because he was talented. Go, Mike's mom!

So, every day for the next month—long past the day he retook his missed test and brought his grade up to passing—Mike and his mama came into my classroom before school. She quizzed him on vocabulary, and when she felt that he knew the words, she made him help me run off copies.

I learned a lot from Mike's mama. She knew her son was talented—but she knew that talent would only take him so far. So she was willing to sacrifice his dreams of a Division I scholarship in order to make sure his heart was right. Because she knew that the easy way certainly wouldn't bring her son success in the things that really mattered.

I hope I would choose the same thing Mike's mom did in that situation. Because I want my kids to grow up with hearts that seek God, not hearts that seek their own fame or talent or success. The good news is that Mike did end up passing my class and getting that college scholarship—but I'm guessing the lessons he learned from his mama in that month when he was failing my class have taken him much farther than any class he's taken in college.

Savvy Mom Takeaways

- ᶜ No matter how much you paid to give your kid an opportunity, don't let it take priority over his heart.
- ᶜ Practices and games are important—but not more important than your kid. If it's not working, skip a day or two.
- ᶜ Pray continuously that God will give you the abilities to prioritize what's most important in your kid's life.

Urban Mom Legend #7: After-game snack bags must have a theme.

The Facts: Did you know that banana halves and juice boxes just don't cut it for after-game snacks anymore? I learned this lesson the hard way after signing up to bring snacks to Joey's first soccer game. The mom in charge of drinks brought tiny Gatorade bottles and matching twisty straws in bags decorated with the team colors, and I brought... orange slices. When I was a kid, I loved a good after-game orange slice or two. But kids these days? They expect full-on swag bags after their Little League games.

Anyway, not wanting to be labeled as the slacker mom, I signed up for snacks for the next game and spent all week strategizing. I bought light-blue paper sacks and filled them with little bags of blueberries and strawberries (get it—the team colors?) and then added a page of stickers, a granola bar, and a napkin to each bag. And the kids loved them. And I was out a whopping sixty-eight bucks for after-game snacks. Compared to the four dollars I spent on oranges the week before, it was quite the blow to my grocery budget.

There's a lot of pressure for extras in extracurriculars these days. And while all of the cute little bear pals and team spirit signs are fun, they certainly aren't important enough for you to stress over. Or kill your grocery budget over. You may not believe this, but your kid and all his friends will probably survive if you bring apple slices with plain white napkins as the after-game snack. And if anyone asks where the personalized fruit snacks are, you can just tell them that I told you not to bring them. They can e-mail me. I'll tell them what I think of their blue-and-orange spirit bags.

Savvy Mom Takeaways

∽ Sign up for the first game and set the bar low. I have a feeling the other parents will be relieved when you show up with orange slices, as it will take the pressure off of everyone else.

- Remind your kid that he plays for the fun of the game—not for the special snacks.

Urban Mom Legend #8: Tooling around at home doesn't build essential skills.

The Facts: When I heard my friend telling me how she had finally scored her daughter a coveted spot in a Spanish-language immersion summer camp, I felt a twinge of jealousy. I mean, the closest my kids get to being bilingual is through watching Dora. And I had a moment of panic that my kids would fall behind in school and life if they didn't have access to amazing cultural and artistic and athletic opportunities every moment of every day.

But after calling the bilingual summer camp (the waiting list was eighty-eight kids long), I had a moment of reason when I realized that my kids would be just fine without a fancy language-immersion program. It's not that art camps and music lessons and sports leagues aren't great things—they are—but they aren't essential things. And if you have the time and money and desire to afford these experiences for your kid, then by all means, sign him up! But if you don't, that's okay too.

Even if your best attempt at art lessons involves Crayola markers and stencils, your kid will still learn about color pairings and that mom doesn't know how to stay in the lines. As far as sports goes—your kid would probably love an afternoon game of soccer in your backyard or going biking around the neighborhood. And music? Even if you can't carry a tune, I'd be willing to bet that that shower-side concerto you put on this morning will be long remembered. Don't discount yourself as a teacher, coach, and instructor. Your kid can learn a lot from you.

Savvy Mom Takeaways

- Your kid is learning and gaining skills just by coloring

pictures or reading books or playing outside. Do your best to give him time to just learn.

- ∽ If your kid shows special abilities in a certain area, encourage it. Turn on the radio and sing along with your budding musician. Buy sidewalk chalk and let your little artist draw.
- ∽ You don't have to spend a fortune to give your kid opportunities. Be creative.

My Last Words Before Setting You (and Your Minivan) Loose on the Soccer Field

You can just call me Lil' Miss Snopes. Because I've done all the dirty work for you—figuring out that Michael Phelps wasn't born swimming, and that those color-coordinated water bottles that you're tempted to spend $235 on are really completely unnecessary. (Because I bet you couldn't have figured that out by yourself.)

So now all you have left to do is load up that minivan with six foam fingers, two blankets, four stadium chairs, a cooler of Gatorade (for you, not your kid), a whistle, some extra shoes, and a partridge in a pear tree and head out to the big game. Or the big concert. Or the big robot-making contest. Or whatever it is that tickles your kid's fancy. This week, at least.

FOURTEEN

Do This, Not That

*Helping Your Kid in a Way
That's Actually Helpful*

I love the book *Eat This, Not That!* There's something about having someone smarter than me tell me to choose the skinny sugar-free latte over the triple java-chip Frappuccino with whip that makes me feel empowered. And like I know something that those other coffee drinkers don't. (Because the average person may not know that a 32-ounce drink smothered in chocolate and whipped cream is bad for you.) It's just nice to have someone tell me what to do sometimes.

And I have to say that navigating being a grade school mom is a lot like ordering at Starbucks—there's a lot of cranky, caffeine-starved people staring at you as you try to figure out why exactly "large" and "venti" are synonymous—and a whole lot on the line if you make the wrong decisions. (Imagine your day if you inadvertently order a "tall." Yikes!) Same goes for being a grade-school mom. Even if you know what you want, it can be a bit tricky to figure out exactly how to get there.

I wish there was a "Do This, Not That" website for parents. It could be sort of like a choose-your-own-adventure book, only you put in the things your kids do and it tells you exactly what to do to make sure your kids are on the right track. Wouldn't that be cool? Maybe someday, after my kids graduate and I have nothing better to do than sit around at Starbucks all day and sip nonfat vanilla lattes without whip, I'll do that. In the meantime, I've put together a few "do this" ideas to help you know exactly how to help you and your kid survive—and love—grade school.

Do Questions, Not Answers

I hate to break it to you, but you already graduated from kindergarten. You learned your letters, how to play nice with others, and even—if you're lucky—how to count from one to ten. I'm guessing you've even retained most of your learning—which means you remember to share your toys (read: iPad) when you really, really don't want to. (Yes, even when things are getting good on Words With Friends.) You did it. And somewhere in your mom's attic, there's probably a fancy-schmancy diploma to prove it.

Now it's your kid's turn. To learn his letters and numbers and how to take turns on the swings at the playground. And while you can and should do everything you can to help him, you also need to keep in mind that your kid's behavior and learning are his responsibility. You can't do it for him. And that means even if you know with 100 percent certainty that C-A-T does indeed spell *cat*, you should probably let him do his own homework on his own. Without you giving him the answers.

My rule for myself—I need to make rules in situations like this in order to keep my perfectionism in check—is that I answer all questions with questions. So, if my kid asks me how to spell *cat*, I say something like, "Well, what sound does *cat* start with?" and then see if he can figure it out by himself. I lead with questions—and give him the chance to come up with his own answers.

Do Mistakes, Not Corrections

I confess: I cringe when Joey answers a question wrong on his homework. And when I notice that he's spelled *cat* with a k-a-t, the first thing I want to do is grab an eraser and fix it. I think it's the writer in me—or maybe it's my totally obsessive perfectionism—but I hate the idea of him turning in less-than-perfect work. But my mom—yes, my mom again—reminds me often that mistakes are learning opportunities. And if I swoop in and correct my kids' mistakes each time they make one, I'm robbing them of the chance to learn. Ouch.

I'll admit, this killed me the first time Joey finished a homework assignment and I could hardly read the words because he crunched them all together on the page. But I let him turn that paper in. And I acted surprised when it came back from the teacher with a note to redo it with "finger spaces" between each word. But Joey redid that assignment that night and, ever since then, he has been diligent to add appropriate spacing between words. I'm guessing my nagging wouldn't have been nearly as effective.

I'm not telling you never to correct your kid's work. If your kid asks you to check his homework, then by all means check it and help him make it better. But don't pounce on every mistake you notice. Instead, give your kid the chance to fix things himself. Have him double-check his own assignments and assess them himself. And yes, at times, it's okay to just let mistakes happen and allow your kid to turn in work that's not on level with what you would've done. Because getting a low grade on an assignment—or worse, having to redo an assignment—can be the best teacher of all.

Do Building Up, Not Blaming

A few weeks ago we had our fall conference with Joey's teacher. She went over everything he'd been doing with his reading and math and then casually mentioned an incident where he had used his little patootie to bump a kid out of line. The teacher saw it and asked Joey to step to the back of the line. Simple enough. But Joey didn't think it was so simple. He wanted his spot in line. And so he argued with his teacher in front of the rest of the class. So heatedly that the teacher finally had to remove him from the classroom.

I was mortified. And my first impulse was to defend myself to his teacher. To explain to her that *I* would never have been disrespectful to a teacher and that *I* had taught him from the time he was a little kid that he needed to respect adults and to tell her that he'd never ever say anything but "yes ma'am" to her again if *I* had anything to do with it. But his teacher stopped me. She put her hand on my arm and said, "Erin, I'm not telling you this to judge you. Kids try things. I'm telling you this so we can help Joey together."

Now, I'm not one to pass the blame (unless, of course, it involves blaming my husband for being late to church, again)—but your kid's behavior isn't your fault. You aren't the one pushing or hitting or whining or blatantly disrespecting the teacher. And while it's easy to internalize the things your kid says and does and wonder if you could possibly have done anything differently, let me reassure you: you could've. There is always something you could've done better to help your kid. But that doesn't make it your fault that he decides to act the wrong way.

I can (almost) guarantee you that whatever your kid has done has probably been done by other kids before. Actually, strike that. I can guarantee you that it's been done by my kid before. And as embarrassing as it can be when our kids do the wrong thing, it's not your job to judge or cringe or blame. It's your job to help.

Just so I can redeem myself a little (I'm still mortified that he talked back to his teacher), I want you to know that we worked with Joey's teacher to come up with a plan that allowed no tolerance for disrespect. If Joey's teacher tells him something, he says, "Yes ma'am," and if he feels that he wants to clarify what he's feeling (ie, argue), he can do it in writing by drafing a letter to the teacher later. If he chooses to argue verbally during class time, his teacher writes a little check in his folder and then reminds him that class time isn't the appropriate time. And if he gets a check mark in his folder, well, then my husband and I deal with that at home later in the evening.

So far our plan has worked, and we haven't had any more back-talking issues at school—thank goodness. But more than just working to stop the disrespect, it has also allowed me to let go of some of the guilt and worry and embarrassment that came with knowing my kid was acting in a way that I would never condone. Because I'm being proactive to help my kid learn appropriate behaviors. And hopefully, helping him to grow into the man that God intends for him to be.

Do Empowerment, Not Bailouts

Joey's kindergarten class did book reports. Okay, so they were more like book "pictures," but regardless, Joey worked really, really hard on his, and he was really, really proud of it. So once he finally finished, I looked over his work and told him how great he had done and then told him to run and put the report in his backpack so we could get ready for bed. And off he went. And—crazy mommy—I assumed that since he had left with his book report and came back without it, he had probably put said book report into his backpack. But I was wrong. The book report was put in the drawer in the laundry room with the dryer sheets. Because why wouldn't it be?

Needless to say, the next morning we (both) had a total meltdown. The book report had disappeared, and while both of us frantically turned the house upside down looking, I silently considered how I could reproduce the book report to look like the one Joey had done. Because after Joey had worked so hard on it, I didn't want him to have to show up at school on book report day without a book report.

Just then my mom walked into my house to pick Joey up to take him to school. I tearily told her what had happened, and she (calmly) told me that it wasn't that big a deal. Not that big a deal?! Didn't she know that Joey had spent a good hour working on it? And that he had used colored pencils and crayons and spelled every word in the title right? It was a huge deal! Okay, so I might have been overreacting. Joey was in kindergarten. His missing book report was probably not going to factor into his SAT scores or his college admissions packet or even into his ability to move on to first grade. The stakes of not turning it in were pretty low. Technically my mom was right: the missing book report was not going to make or break Joey.

My mom and I sat Joey down on the couch and asked him what he thought he could do to fix the situation. His first response was that I could call his teacher and tell him that someone had lost it and that it was done and maybe he could just give him a good grade for trying. But when I vetoed that (for some reason I didn't want to be *that* mom, having *that* conversation with his teacher), Joey came up with a plan all on his own: he was going to write a note to the teacher, explaining that his book report was done but he lost it. And then he was going to spend at least an hour looking for the book report that night and turn it in one day late.

Joey quickly wrote his note and headed off to school with his note in hand. I got a call from his teacher later that day, telling me that he totally understood and that he was so proud of Joey for taking responsibility instead of making excuses. That night, when Joey got home, we looked for the report together and (eventually) found it. And guess what? He still passed kindergarten. He still has a snazzy kindergarten diploma on our refrigerator. And he learned a pretty good lesson about responsibility to boot. (Not to mention the importance of putting things away in his backpack instead of in the laundry room.)

Do "Organized," Not "Personal Maid"

I like things to be done a certain way. It's not that I can't be flexible, per se, but considering the fact that my methods are clearly the best methods, it only makes sense to do things my way. And so, for months during the last school year, I carried the kids' backpacks in from the car, emptied them onto the counter, and sorted through the cracker crumbs and homework assignments and permission slips to figure out what exactly we needed to get done each night.

It took a lot of time and effort on my part—but let's just say that no one ever lost an assignment or missed a field trip permission slip. But they also never caught on to the fact that their backpacks didn't empty and reorganize themselves every night. Or that if they put an old sandwich in the hidden back pocket of the bag, no one was going to notice it and take it out until it started to smell. I wasn't doing them any favors by organizing their lives for them.

So I decided to try an organizational system I found on Pinterest. I hung hooks on a wall in my laundry room—one hook for Joey's bag, one for his coat, and one for his lunch box. Then, above the hooks, I hung clipboards. One is labeled "homework" and another "for mom" and another "stuff I want you to see." When Joey and Kate get home from school, their job is to hang their backpacks on the hooks and then to bring their lunch boxes to the kitchen. After that, they go through their backpacks and clip homework to the "homework" board and permission slips and whatnot to the "for mom" board. They also hang any work that has been completed onto the "stuff I want you to see" board so I can ooh and aah over it later.

I can't say the system has worked perfectly—there have been several times when homework assignments and old sandwiches have slipped through the cracks. But overall, I'm liking it. It's not my way—but it's a way. A way for them to learn to organize their lives and their school stuff that's doable for them. Without my having to be their personal maid in the process.

Do This, Not That

I have to say that I'm kind of liking telling you what to do. And while I'm at it, I should probably tell you that next time you're at the coffee shop, you should totally try one of those salted caramel mochas. (Just go with the grande size instead of the venti—I think someone told me that's better for you.) But I also thought I'd finish off this chapter—and this book—with a list of things you should do to empower your kids to be the people that God wants them to be. And while this is obviously oversimplified—there's no list of "to-dos" that can help you raise your kids right—I hope it will encourage you as you start your years as a big-kid mom and help you find the vision for what you want yourself—and your family—to become.

- Live your faith—your kid is watching you, and your actions say much more than your words.
- Trust God in everything—He is the giver of all hope, and He has a perfect plan for both you and your kid.
- Think ahead—enjoy today, but look forward to a future that aspires to reach God's plan.
- Don't give up—no matter what the setback or failure, God will use it to make you stronger.
- Pray before you act—allow God to influence your decisions and guide your path.
- Work hard and smart—raising kids takes work, and it's okay to put some elbow grease into it. Just be sure to put some "knee" grease into it as well. Intercede for your kids in prayer every day.
- Stop blaming—everyone has fallen short of the glory of God, but everyone has also been given the opportunity to come to God for forgiveness.
- Look at others through God's eyes—He gives each of us grace that far outweighs our deservedness. Imagine how wonderful life would be if we afforded each other (and our kids!) the same luxury.
- Read the Bible every day—and find ways to share the truths you learn with your kids.

- Be willing to listen and learn from others—even your kids.
- Be honest—both in your words and with yourself.
- Love joyfully and fully—even when it hurts or your pride tells you to run the other way. Love covers a multitude of sins.
- Hope fully—God has given you everything you need to survive and thrive both as a mother and as a person. Put your hope in Him, and He will carry you to the places He wants you to go.

Epilogue

Bring on the Big-Kidness

I'm going to get a bit hyper-sentimental on you here for a minute. Because that's what writers do when they're finished with a book and feel that they need to send their readers off with some inspiring and powerful words. Well, that and I'm feeling a bit teary today because it's Kate's fifth birthday. In fact, in just a few minutes, we're heading out the door to go out to Red Lobster—her choice, not ours—to celebrate. And tonight, as she guzzles down that shrimp scampi and opens that Dream Lites unicorn she's been asking for, I'll paste on my biggest smile and smother her with hugs as I try to hide the bittersweet tears that are sure to creep up behind my eyes.

This morning, when I woke her up by singing "Happy Birthday" at the top of my lungs, the first tear slid down my face. Kate looked at me with her big, brown eyes and said, "Mommy, you can still love me when I'm five, you know?" And she's right—nothing has changed today just because she has five years under her belt. I still love her just as much as I did yesterday—probably more. But my mommy-sentimentality kicks in when I look at my beautiful blessing of a daughter and think of who she is and—more important—who God is shaping her to become.

Kate wasn't born strong. She was born tiny and frail, and as a result of a difficult pregnancy, she struggled to grow and thrive for her first two years. In fact, at just twelve days old, she was admitted into the NICU as doctors helped her overcome an infection that her tiny body just couldn't fight. But she did fight—then, and countless other times during those first few years. She fought to grow. She fought to thrive. She's fighting to become the person God intended for her to be. And now, when I look back on Kate's tenuous start, I am in awe of my daughter. Because she may not have been born strong, but she *is* strong.

Physically, Kate has caught up to her peers both in strength and size—you should see the girl play soccer—but I'm more concerned about spiritual strength. And God has grown her into the kind of kid who I am proud to call my daughter. She's kind. She's generous. She's tenacious. She's honest. And she's empathetic. All qualities that I pray God will continue to grow in her in the next year. Make that *years*.

What's more, Kate is strong enough to know who she is. Okay, she's five, so she certainly doesn't know which political candidates she's rooting for or which theological issues are hot buttons for her, but she's growing a sense of who she is every day. She knows that she loves Jesus—and that part of loving Jesus means choosing the right thing, even when it's not easy. She knows she comes from a family that values tradition and honesty and respect and love. And she knows she has cousins and siblings and friends to lean on when things get tough.

Tonight, when she blows out the candles on her carrot cake (that I bought and moved onto a china plate because I didn't feel like baking . . . *shh!*), I will be silently praying for her. Praying that this year will bring her a sense of joy that can only come from having a childlike faith and a sense of trust that can only come from knowing who she is in Christ. Oh, and also that she'd stop growing so fast, because I'm getting a bit tired of buying her new shoes every two months.

As my precious, only daughter stands on the brink of big-kidness,

I pray that I can be the mom she needs as she steps out into the big, wide world. Because the The Fifteen Factors skills don't learn themselves. And those feet won't stop growing just because I will them to. I want my kids to always know who they are, and that, as children of God, they are not only cherished and loved, but they have a hope and a future that is better than any of us can even begin to imagine.

Appendix

*The Christian Mama's Guide
to Praying for Your Kids*

To my Christian Mama friends,

There is such power in praying for our kids! As a mom, there are many days that I feel desperate—desperate for more sleep, more patience, more time, more go-to recipes that my kids will eat without melting down. And while my natural inclination is always to try to fix things myself, I'm learning that the only path to peace and hope is by going directly to my Savior.

I can't even begin to go in-depth about the power of prayer—that's an entire bookshelf of books in itself—but I do want to finish this book by sharing some of the things I've learned about prayer. I'm fortunate because I was raised by prayer warriors. My grandmother, Kerttu, and my mom, Ellen, both kneel before the King daily to ask for His provision in my life. Additionally, God has blessed me with some wonderful, praying friends and mentors who have truly blessed me by teaching me how to go to my God in prayer.

Anyway, I want to encourage you to start (or to continue) praying daily for your kids in a way that's purposeful and scripture-based. And I hope that the verses, ideas, and thoughts I share in the next few pages can help in some small way. I'd love to hear how you pray for your kids as well—email me at erin@christian-mamasguide.com—I'm always looking to learn more about prayer.

Blessings,

Erin

Lessons from an Octogenarian Prayer Warrior

Ever since I was a little girl, I knew my precious grandmother, Mummu, was praying for me. She prayed for me every morning—out loud and on her knees—and throughout each and every day. I was so comforted knowing that no matter where I was or what I was doing, someone out there was going to my Father for me.

A few weeks ago, my mom, realizing that Mummu's habit of daily prayer had led to a close and intimate relationship with God, asked Mummu how she prays. Mummu pulled a well-worn sheet out of her prayer journal that was entitled *Koinka Rukoilla* (How to Pray). The page—written decades ago in Mummu's native Finnish language—described my grandmother's prayer strategy in her own words. She told my mom that she wrote and rewrote this page, and has now been reading and rereading it for decades.

My mom was kind enough to translate Mummu's *Koinka Rukoilla* into English for me and I'd love to share it with you here. This is how my eighty-five-year-old prayer warrior of a grandmother prays:

> Go to the Lord in humility and bow before Him *on your knees*.
> Be alone with God.
> Be mindful that He alone is God; He will accomplish all His work.
> Surrender. Wait.
> The Holy Spirit is your helper given to you by God Himself.
> Learn from Him.
> Be still. Listen.
> He will hear you and help you, *unless* you harbor wrong thoughts about others or allow bitterness to remain in your heart.
> Listen to others. But be alone with God.
> That will be best for you.
> Listen. Learn.
> Do all of your battling on your knees!!

Praying Scripture for Your Kids

My amazing MOPS mentor mom Sharmon Coleman shared with me a list of verses that she uses to pray for her daughters. I love this! Using God's word as a starting place as I pray has really helped me to pray specifically and intentionally for my kids. And so I want to share Sharmon's list—along with several of my own additions—that I have used to pray for my kids over the past year.

Verses to read when you're praying for your kids' salvation and redemption

- **Psalm 63:1**—*That my kids would learn to honestly seek Him*
- **John 1:12**—*That my kids would become children of God*
- **John 14:6**—*That my kids will know God as the only way, truth, and life*
- **Romans 1:16**—*That the power of Christ would be at work in my kids' hearts and lives*
- **2 Corinthians 5:17**—*That my kids would become new creatures in Him*
- **Ephesians 2:8**—*That my kids would know God's saving grace*
- **Ephesians 2:9**—*That my kids would fully understand that salvation is a gift and not a result of their own works*
- **1 John 3:2**—*That as my kids mature, they would see God for who and what he truly is*
- **1 John 2:1-29**—*That my kids would truly know Christ*

Verses to read when you're praying for your kids' personal and spiritual growth

- **Romans 12:1-2**—*That my kids would learn to give themselves fully to Christ*

- **Psalm 97:10**—*That my kids would develop a hatred for sin*
- **Proverbs 1:10**—*That my kids would be able to resist pressure to do wrong from friends and peers*
- **I Corinthians 6:18-20**—*That my kids would remain pure, both in heart and in body*
- **1 Peter 4:13**—*That my kids would grow closer to God through their trials*
- **Daniel 6:3**—*That my kids would have good mentors that teach them personal and spiritual responsibility*
- **1 Peter 2:1-25**—*That my kids would crave right and resist wrong*
- **Philippians 1:9-11**—*That my kids would grow in knowledge and discernment every day*
- **Psalm 119:105**—*That my kids would rely on God's Word*

Verses to read when you're praying for your kids' future

- **II Corinthians 6:14-17**—*That my kids would seek purity and holiness in their lives*
- **Hosea 2:6**—*That God would protect my kids from bad influences*
- **John 17:15**—*That my kids would be protected from the evil one*
- **Proverbs 16:9**—*That God would walk alongside my kids as they grow and learn*
- **Isaiah 40:31**—*That my kids would depend wholeheartedly on God*

Verses to read when you're praying for yourself as a mom

- **1 Timothy 3:15**—*That I would set an example of what it means to live in truth*
- **Psalm 37**—*That I would learn to be still and trust in God's provision*

- **Matthew 7:3-6**—*That I would avoid hypocrisy and show my kids what it means to follow Christ*
- **Psalm 16:11**—*That God would guide my path as a mom*
- **Ephesians 6:18**—*That I would form the habit of coming before my God in prayer daily and continually*
- **Titus 2:1-15**—*That I would set a godly example for my kids*
- **Proverbs 31:10-12**—*That I would fulfill the role God gave me as a wife and mother*
- **Ephesians 5:25-28**—*That my marriage relationship would set a godly example to my kids*
- **Ephesians 6:4**—*That I would guide my children with a compassionate heart instead of a critical heart*
- **Ecclesiastes 3:1-17**—*That I would recognize God's timing in all things*

To My Christian Mama Friends

Thank you for taking this journey with me! And as you face big-kidness and beyond, I pray that God will sprinkle your words with His truth and your actions with grace. Because without Him, we cannot be the parents our kids need.

I've love to hear from you! Please drop by my website at www.christianmamasguide.com or e-mail me at erin@ christianmamasguide.com and we can continue this conversation together.

In Him, Erin

About the Author

Erin MacPherson is a mom of three who wants to come beside her readers not only as a confidante and Christian sister, but also as a friend who understands what it's like to juggle kids, life, and a much-too-messy house. When she discovered she was pregnant she decided to write about it—but then kept writing. A former staff writer and editor for Nickelodeon, Erin now entertains parents on her personal blog, www.christianmamasguide.com, as well as through her staff writing job with WeAreTeachers.com, freelance magazine articles, devotionals and speaking. Erin, her assistant principal husband Cameron, and her kids Joey (7), Kate (5), and Will (1) live in Austin, Texas.

About Ellen Schuknecht

Ellen Schuknecht has been working as an educator for more than thirty-five years, with experience ranging from early childhood education to high school advising to family ministries counseling. She currently serves as the dean of family ministries at Veritas Academy in Austin, Texas, where she mentors parents, teachers, and students on a daily basis. She uses her blog, www.familywings.org, as well as her many speaking engagements as a platform to help parents learn how to lead their children to Christ in a way that's not only authentic, but that also builds the relationship between parent and child. Ellen has been married to her husband Glen for thirty-eight years and lives in Austin, Texas, near her three grown children, their spouses, and—her pride and joy—nine precious grandchildren ranging in age from "due any day" to seven.

Index